Parenting and Delinquent Youth

Alice Parizeau
University of Montreal

Translated by
Dorothy R. Crelinsten

LexingtonBooks
D.C. Heath and Company
Lexington, Massachusetts
Toronto

Library of Congress Cataloging in Publication Data

Parizeau, Alice Poznanska, 1930-
    Parenting and delinquent youth.

    Bibliography: p.
    1. Juvenile delinquency—Québec (Province)—Montreal—Case studies.
2. Children—Legal status, laws, etc.—Québec (Province)—Montreal.
3. Children's rights—Québec (Province)—Montreal. 4. Juvenile delinquency—Prevention. 5. Family social work. I. Title.
HV9110.M66P37   364.3'6'09714281   79-47982
ISBN 0-669-03620-x

Published simultaneously in Canada.

Printed in the United States of America.

International Standard Book Number: 0-669-03620-x

Library of Congress Catalog Card Number: 79-47982

Parenting and
Delinquent Youth

Contents

List of Figures
and Tables

Figures

Tables

Preface

In presenting this work to the American reader, we believe some remarks are in order. The book is an analysis of two studies conducted in Montreal on the progress of certain minors through the justice system. Similar dossiers are to be found in the juvenile courts in the United States. Thus, the realities are comparable. What emerges, in my opinion, is a certain weakness in the justice system—an inability to adequately solve the problems of children who lack sufficient family support.

This brings us to the treatment of underprivileged or delinquent children. In dealing with prevention, we should ask ourselves, along with the Gluecks and many other American sociologists, whether or not it is imperative that the family receive both financial aid and, above all, educational assistance. The major difficulty is selecting the families for whom such aid should be a priority. In this study an effort has been made to measure the type of life and methods of transmitting values adopted by a group of recidivist prisoners. The book contains a list of the prisoners' answers to a questionnaire and their comments during interviews.

However, we should not conclude from these data that intervention ought to be concentrated solely on the families of delinquent recidivists who have children. It is obvious that there are too many variables for us to adopt such a standard approach. What seems important to me is that studies dealing with delinquent parents are relatively less numerous than those that concern delinquent minors, although these are the families that should have priority.

According to the legislation that prevails in our society, because of blood ties, children belong to their parents body and soul. The question raised in this book is whether it is not more important to do away with the myth that parental love can compensate for all the lacks of the parents, instead of focusing on the behavior of the children. It is from this point of view that we should consider the reform of certain laws.

The results of this research are representative of a school of thought being accepted in other countries and particularly by American researchers, some of whose inquiries and evaluations are analyzed in this work.

Introduction

Children are the future citizens of the world, but this fact is hardly reflected in legislation. Laws were not based on the concept that the greatest natural resource of any community is its children, but rather were designed to regulate relationships between and among citizens and to control crime.

The laws concerning children, therefore, are found in the section concerning the family in our civil code, in our statutory laws, and in the Canadian Criminal Code.

The Quebec civil code dates back to 1866. It recognizes religious marriage, which it considers irreversible, and hence rejects divorce. It accepts the inferiority of the natural child and stresses the diverse aspects of paternal authority. More generally, the civil code contains laws to protect the continuation of the family, the absolute authority of the father, and the right of the legitimate child to inherit.

However, with the changes that occurred at the time of the Quiet Revolution, that is, following the 1960s, a number of reforms were introduced. Thus in 1964, Bill 16, on the emancipation of the married woman, was adopted; in 1968-1969, the matrimonial laws were revised, civil marriages were recognized, and a new law was introduced on divorce and adoption. In addition, in 1970, Bill 48 gave certain rights to the natural child.

The Civil Code Review Board (l'Office de Révision du Code Civil) has recently submitted a report proposing several reforms with regard to the legislation concerning the child and the family. The project has not yet been discussed at the government level, but it is by all evidence much more in conformity with the present sociocultural reality and is a major work in itself.

Concerning the statutory law, since the beginning of the century the Quebec lawmaker has had in view the protection of the disadvantaged child. The laws contained in the Revised Statutes of Quebec of 1909, 1925, and 1941 are designed to give charitable institutions a basis on which to legitimize their handling of "foundlings, and orphans, who lead a life of vagabondage," as well as those "who are habitually beaten or cruelly treated by their parents or the persons with whom they live."[1]

The Act for the Protection of Youth would later on include a number of articles that had already been passed during this period, although its philosophy would be considered new back in 1964, or even now, at the moment of its complete revision. In fact, what is most important about Bill 24 and is only beginning to be applied is its emphasis on the social approach and social autonomy as compared with judicial treatment.

With regard to the criminal responsibility of minors, it starts at the age of seven "and even before," according to the Canadian Juvenile Delinquents Act, which is still in force. Let us compare this with Sweden, where the age limit is fifteen years, or other European countries, where the lawmakers have gradually raised it to thirteen and fourteen.

The dichotomy between the legislation for the protection of minors and the "treatment" of juvenile delinquents theoretically places minors in two categories: children in need of protection and children who are delinquents. This is sheer hypocrisy today, for in Quebec, as in many other countries, these categories are hardly ever respected when a child is placed in an institution. In principle, institutional placement is meant solely for "difficult," "uncontrollable," and in general, delinquent children. In practice, however, the question of family support is crucial in this regard.

Thus a child of twelve found guilty of several thefts, whose father intervenes, reimburses the victim, and offers every guarantee to persuade the police, social workers, and judges that he will control his son in future, can avoid placement in an institution. Objectively speaking, this could be called "class justice," but the fact remains that it is also a logical way of saving the taxpayer money. Since juvenile delinquents are no longer punished, but are placed in institutions to be "resocialized," it is just as well after a warning to entrust this task to the family and not uselessly burden the services whose results are in any case constantly being questioned.

Similarly, the child whose parents are cruel, indifferent, or criminals receives no help from the community as long as he does not prove troublesome. Social workers have strict directives in this regard. Placement outside the home is never recommended except when there is no other solution. Under this system, the ten-year-old petty thief or the young prostitute of twelve can continue to carry on an existence that completely distorts their character until they become hardened, attempt a major offence, and are arrested. During this time, they can be ill-treated at home and rejected by the school and their peers, but no effective help will be forthcoming. Considering the lack of space and the quality of the services available, it is better to wait, for in any case the results of preventive policies have never been proven valid; they merely stigmatize youngsters who can eventually reform themselves. Who knows? Children grow up and change.

Very true, or a rationalization dreamed up by the community to save it the painful duty of becoming involved in defiance of the rights of parents, infinitely better defined in the codes than the rights of children. Better to do nothing than do the wrong thing.

In this regard, the Swedish system is exceptional, for a child is not responsible under the law until the age of fifteen, until which time he can be taken in charge only by the social services. In other words, the Swedes, instead of evolving gradually, introduced a radical change.

In effect, at the beginning of the century, all children whose behavior did not conform to the basic norms of society were considered delinquents under the law. Subsequently, an effort was made to limit the age, and the system of law enforcement was changed, giving broad discretionary powers to social workers, the police, and judges. The Swedes reversed this trend completely. All disadvantaged, rejected, or delinquent children were considered to be in need of protection. Only after the age of fifteen could they be referred to a court of justice, but the judges had the power to refuse to hear the case and return the young person to the care of the social services. As a result, assistance and treatment of the adolescent no longer bears a stigma; this makes it easier to intervene both before and after the age of puberty, since biologically it is during this latter period, especially for boys, that crucial changes in character can occur.

If we take for granted that society does not want to use repression, but rather education in the case of juvenile delinquency, it would be well to recognize that this approach has a greater chance of success. Young people are more malleable, and it is easier to inculcate proper modes of behavior in a child than in an adolescent who has already been marked by a number of bad experiences.

In Quebec, the norms for the application of Bill 24 seem to be oriented toward increased social treatment rather than what is defined as judicial treatment, if only because of the powers given the directors of the child protection services. Federal legislation concerning juvenile delinquency, however, still makes a distinction between child protection and juvenile delinquency, and this starts at the age of seven, or even before. This means that minors are subjected to a sort of sinister game that goes on between social worker and judge. In effect, the system permits the social services, when unable to settle a case, to send it before the judge, who then returns it to the same services for the execution of his sentence.

It is true, however, that although an appearance before the court leaves a stigma, it also serves as a warning to the child and his parents. Individual rights also are better protected by a court than by social workers, whose training often leaves much to be desired and whose professional responsibility is practically nil. A judge, on the other hand, must motivate and sign his sentence, which can be appealed should the need arise.

All these arguments are valid in themselves, but they can be refuted. For example, facilitating the procedures necessary to appeal the decisions of social workers before the juvenile courts would suffice to eliminate a good many possibilities for arbitrary judgments. It would also eliminate a good many possibilities for arbitrary options. However, this game of sending the child from the social services to the courts involves delays of several months, if not years. When the judge finally passes judgment, he is asked to "resocialize" the minor, whereas it is actually too late by this time to undertake any effective measures.

Contrary to the system that prevailed earlier, the judge now has only the same options as the social worker and is mainly concerned with conflicts between adults. When the social worker can no longer handle a case, it is the judge who assumes the unwelcome task of rendering a decision, and it is also he who must settle any conflict that arises between the social worker and the parents over what should be done with their child.

Juvenile judges in Quebec hear more than 35,000 cases every year. However, to get an exact idea of the total number of children urgently in need of preventive measures, it is necessary to consider the statistics of both the juvenile courts and the social services. According to the last report of the Quebec Department of Welfare, two million youths under 18 years of age were evaluated. Of this total, 30,000 were considered in need of care outside their family homes for various periods. This does not mean that this is the total number of children who may be in need of care.

The Protection of Minors and the Responsibilities of the Parents

In this area, the question arises as to where the responsibilities of the parents stop and those of the child begin as far as his or her actions and behavior are concerned. To date, no one has been able to answer this question, and legislators are limited to a definition of extreme cases, such as appear in the criminal codes providing for the forfeiture of parents' rights. This concept does not exist in Canada, but juvenile judges can forbid parents the right to see a child of theirs who is placed in a foster home or an institution, either for a limited or undetermined period.[2] Anglo-Saxon tradition, always empiric, veers away from global solutions, preferring to leave the magistrate the discretion necessary to evaluate each case on its own merits.

On the human and social side, the problem is much more complex than from the legal point of view, for no one has yet succeeded in clearly defining the meaning of such a simple term as *good parents*. We have succeeded in measuring exactly how much water and fertilizer is needed for a plant to grow, but so far we have not been able to estimate, even approximately, what is necessary for the harmonious development of the human body and mind.

This has not prevented certain American doctors from making a fortune by developing theories whose publication made millions of women feel guilty. These doctors tried to define parental love through certain daily actions, absurd in their simplicity, upon which, according to them, depended healthy growth. Without the slightest sense of humor, these specialists presented conclusions based on more or less reliable data.

Although it is possible to measure the needs of the child in terms of food and hygiene, each human being is an individual. Moreover, love cannot be evaluated collectively, but only in a highly individualistic way. Furthermore, the very idea of parental love is very uncertain, as are subconscious motivations.

Maternal love, idealized in accordance with Judeo-Christian tradition, is hard to reconcile with the actual indifference of certain mothers who abandon their children as soon as they are no longer influenced by social pressure.

At one time, such mothers were considered monsters; today, those who dare use this label publicly are rare indeed.

Where the training, not the love, of the child is concerned, it has been proved that as the child grows up, the meaning of adult actions and behavior changes. The young human being remembers them, but in a form that does not necessarily coincide with their original intention. Messages received by the mind also vary with the individual. What one child will consider a just reward will be resented by another as a punishment, and by a third as a proof of indifference.

In short, we find many variables in this area, existing at many levels of various scales of conduct, that are almost impossible to measure and compare. Add to this the differences in sociocultural contexts and it will be easily understood that most recipes for the upbringing of children, outside of those based on good commonsense, are, and will be for a long time, only attempts to popularize a science that is too dependent on learned and accepted traditions to be fully valid.

It is obvious that a plant needs sunshine and that a growing human being needs a certain number of hours sleep, but it is utterly impossible in the same way to measure factors related to the transmission of moral values, the rules of living, or progress in the acquisition of knowledge. For lack of scientific models, the emotional motivations of parents are stressed by defining them as sufficiently strong to compensate for everything, including the absence of the most elementary knowledge of accepted behavior patterns.

In the animal world, every species looks after its young, with the exception of a few fish, for example, that devour their young, but the training cycle of the animal is limited in time and consists mainly of learning how to procure the means of subsistence. The geese studied by Konrad Lorenz do not live long enough to see the evolution of two or three cycles of reproduction, but among humans, grandparents and great-grandparents have time to assess the results of the upbringing they have given their children and to live through the conflicts occasioned by the contacts of this upbringing with other factors of community or individual pressure.

There is no proof, furthermore, either for the animal or human species, that the natural parents can give more love, or simply attention, to their offspring than others who decide, for one reason or another, to take their place. What is certain is that among humans the argument of the love of children derives from a form of narcissism, a seeking to compensate for their own imperfections or failures, and a subconscious effort to thwart death.

To have children is theoretically to have the semidivine power to mold, fashion, and bring into existence a being capable of "avenging" the adult's unrealized aspirations and who, in all likelihood, will survive and prolong his or her memory within and beyond the family milieu.

One can consequently be almost led to believe that to love a child is to love oneself. However, many people dislike themselves and may very well be tempted to destroy in their children what appears to them to be signs of resemblance. Taken to the absurd, this could mean that parents who abandon their children love them perhaps too much to impose on them the burden of identification with what they themselves are.

The unmarried mother without any means who gives her child up for adoption loves it perhaps more than the mother who keeps it "to play doll" with, and the same can be applied to the man who refuses to assume paternity because he considers himself incapable of serving as a model to a young person. If we recognize this fluidity of the idea of parental love, however, we can no longer continue to preach the traditional hypothesis that parents by definition love their children and are the only ones who can make them happy.

In addition to the vague notion of love is that of happiness—also impossible to define. Henri Laborit writes with a good bit of cynicism:[3]

> Before wanting to prepare your children to be happy, try if you can, not to participate in creating their unhappiness. It is an act of grace I wish for you, which has little chance of being granted unless your untimely death gives them the opportunity of creating you into a myth which they can then fashion according to their desire [free translation].

I do not go so far as to claim that the best way of assuring the harmonious development of a young person is to make him or her an orphan, but I would like to present three hypotheses that I feel are basic. First, the traditional concept of good parents, based on genetic bonds and by definition upholding the existence of parental love, seems to me refutable at the very least, not having any scientific proof. Second, the upbringing of a child requires that the educator, whether the natural parents or foster parents, have some kind of behavior pattern to transmit. Third, the only fundamental fact that cannot be denied is the recognition that the human being grows up more satisfactorily in an individualized milieu, that is, within a family, than in any communal environment that society can create for him or her.

By the word *culture* I mean a certain number of intuitions or elementary certainties derived from the wisdom of generations and stripped of ideas dictated by more or less passing fashions. This form of culture exists in all societies, but it stems, more or less, from distortions created by the type of life led by the preceding generation.

In his book *L'éloge de la Fuite*, Henri Laborit, doctor, biologist, philosopher and sociologist, writes:[4]

> One might well imagine that it is the entire social group and no longer the family group that assures the protection of the child. He could find just as much security and affection there. He would have the advantage of not being tied to parental individualism, of which the least one can say is that it most often expresses self-admiration on the part of the

middle generation. Unfortunately, it seems that the experiment tried in the kibbutzim in Israel, though encouraging in some respects, is not so in others. The collective group, at least to date, is no more capable than the family group of avoiding the imposition of conformist thinking on the child. There is even some question as to whether family individualism doesn't transmit a polymorphism more to be desired than the collectivism of the group. Rebellion against the father is easier since he is a single entity and not a communal figure. Consequently, the conceptual combination resulting from individuals having grown up and developed in different homes, even if they are all subjected to a dominant ideology, is more likely to generate conflicts, no doubt, but also creativity, than that resulting from the contact of individuals from the same collective environment [free translation].

In this sense, the old adage "Better a family than no family at all" applies, but the latter does not have to be that of parent/offspring; it can be established on the basis of a relationship of foster parent/child.

I emphasize this basic fact because I feel it is important in the planning of social policies concerning minors. The moment it is agreed that parents are capable or incapable of bringing up their children, no matter what their socioeconomic situation and the potential for love they have or think they have, then we must recognize the right of society to intervene, not only a posteriori, but also a priori.

The Community and the Rights of the Individual

Actually, a posteriori intervention has always existed. The community reserves the right to stigmatize and punish those whose degree of social integration is insufficient for them to be able to function in society without causing trouble. One might think that children who have not been brought up to conform sufficiently are automatically rejected by those peers who conform more closely to the requirements of the community. However, the very term *conformism* calls for caution; it is the fashion to use it indiscriminately, no doubt, but this solves nothing.

Over and above the communal ideas and pressures that exist everywhere and in every era, there are elementary rules of social life. These rules are transmitted by the family unit or they are not, and in this sense, there are good or bad parents. Conformism is submission to the predominant norms in a given milieu, group, or community. The rules of life in society consist in having sufficient respect for others not to provoke anyone unless absolutely necessary.

The child who hits his teacher in not a nonconformist, but someone whose upbringing is incomplete, for it does not include the transmission of these fundamental rules. It is here that misunderstandings arise in the evaluation of certain situations concerning children.

The student who, under a dictatorship, opposes the principle of a single party and who, in a democracy, questions that of several parties is a nonconformist. His family environment has inculcated in him a sense of individual reasoning and personal reflection. Moreover, this family milieu wanted to, or was able to, inculcate in him a taste and respect for knowledge.

However, the student whose behavior is an embarrassment to the community because he attacks others and takes or ruins their property is first rejected by the group, then prosecuted and rejected as an undesirable element by the community under the label of "juvenile delinquent."

The misunderstanding comes from confusing the terms and claiming that juvenile delinquents are nonconformists, that is, youngsters whose family has inculcated a tendency to go contrary to that which prevails in the community. Actually, it is generally a question of children whose families did not give them the elements that would enable them to live in the community, whatever their predominant ideologies.

True, the concept of good or bad parents also can be measured by such criteria as the happiness of the child, for as we have already mentioned, there are too many variables that enter here for us to be able to find a valid definition, or simply one that is possible to defend objectively. Whatever the case, studies show that the majority of delinquent children have been brought up by irresponsible, cruel, indifferent, or crime-involved families and that society intervenes in the case of the children, but rarely in the case of parents. The action taken is more or less severe according to the period concerned, but it has always existed in every part of the world. This is intervention a posteriori.

A priori intervention, which consists of evaluating the ability of adults to take care of children, is practically nonexistent in the case of natural parents and rather slow and meddlesome when it comes to adoptive or foster parents. Although no model of good parents has been arrived at to date, every effort is made to slow down the procedures and increase verifications when people want to bring up someone else's child. Generally speaking, a priori intervention, that is, the prevention of childhood misery and deprivation, is widely discussed and sparingly applied.

In today's world, children remain the "property" of their natural parents and cannot be given assistance, in fact, except through them, and mostly by means of financial aid. Families whose incomes are lower than the national average receive a supplementary allowance that varies according to the number of children they have in their charge, but it happens rarely that these children are given support to compensate for the cultural lacks of parents who consequently make them incapable of getting along in other than a marginal group.

Coming back to the example of plants, a stem that is growing in a direction unfavorable to its development will be aided by a prop around which it can twine or which will serve as a support. In the case of children, this very simple idea of prevention is extremely difficult to apply. Mere observation is sufficient to show that the plant needs a support, but who—and by what right—can propose this in the case of a human being? Furthermore, how can the qualifications of those who intervene be defined, and how can their actions be planned administratively without challenging the right of individuals—the natural parents—to handle their children?

We live in an era when we enjoy playing with words because we fear the aggression that action involves. Thus we speak of prevention when a child is confined to a reform school, which has suitably become a school of protection or a training center. Society is no longer punishing its children, it is sheltering and protecting them!

The fact remains that there is a sinister reality hidden behind these terms that constitute mere pious vows. For lack of true prevention inside and outside the school, each generation provides a certain percentage of criminals we are pleased to call marginal. The fact is that they do not live on the margin of society, but on the contrary, live on its cultural acquisitions. They kill, torture, pillage, and steal because the community has possessions and rules of conduct that make a certain type of life easier for them than is generally admitted. They do not organize a life apart from the other members of society; they take advantage of them.

Does this form of exploitation bring them any happiness? Just as it is impossible to define happiness, it is equally obvious that no one dare claim that this type of life is desirable for children. We generally do not cultivate carnivorous or poisonous plants in the house, and parents, watching their children grow up, do not say, "I hope some day he will be a good murderer, a first class thief, or a perfect drug addict and alcoholic."

Childhood per se exists, but it is also a stage, for in the cycle of life it occupies only the first 14 or 15 years, upon which depend all the rest. Childhood is the promise of the future, and the family upbringing fashions this future. Accordingly, the intervention of the community should be directed toward preventing the warping of this future, at least where it seems most predictable. Action taken only at the moment of crisis—whether it is to order a boy of sixteen not to kill any more or not to commit his twentieth robbery or the placement of a child of twelve who has known only criminals all his life, believing that he will then develop as a good citizen—is not prevention; it is the protection of the community against conduct that has become troublesome.

True prevention will never be possible, however, in terms of the population as a whole. Even with the establishment of certain social controls like those practiced in France, England, or Belgium, such as home visits or guardianship in foster families, it will always be difficult to foresee a situation and act in advance. No one will dare decide to systematically intervene in the case of parents who cannot transmit the most elementary social culture, even if it can be predicted that they will fail in their educational role.

A system of prevention can nonetheless be conceived whereby parents having certain sociocultural characteristics could be partially or totally taken in charge, at a time when their children are still very young. Similarly, it is conceivable to promote methods to ensure paraeducative assistance for children during special periods, and thus to facilitate a social integration that is not being achieved by the family. This is not a new or original approach, but rather an attempt to plan under present conditions what was organized, after a fashion, in the past.

During the nineteenth and the beginning of the twentieth century, the clergy and community services of the parish, women doing good works, or patrons used to help numerous families and problem parents in order to compensate their children to some extent. The sudden or gradual withdrawal of these services that occurred in most Western countries showed a lack of appreciation of their just merit. Beneficence was replaced by the individual's right to state assistance, but this aid, which is costing the taxpayer more and more, has had to be limited and regulated in order to respect the rights of individuals and the inviolability of the home.

In Quebec, oddly enough, where socioreligious fervor had been intense, there was an incredibly rapid withdrawal of all community assistance to families and children, making it all the more difficult to set up substitute services. Family individualism, supported and protected by the civil code and other statutory legislation, complied with the advice and pressures of the religious authorities, but would not as easily tolerate the intervention of laymen sent by the justice administration and the social services. It is not surprising, then, that a uniform system of social assistance, unemployment relief, and free hospital care could be set up, but not a system of prevention in families other than financial aid.

Even more, given the cost of such a system, it is obvious that it could only be applied to very limited groups, which implies ipso facto a form of stigmatization. Are we to decree that all single-parent families, for example, should automatically be supervised and assisted by a guardian? Do we dare consider that the children of single-parent families should be systematically protected by society as a preventive measure? Precedents do exist. Swedish law provides that unmarried mothers can keep their child only on condition that a guardian be appointed to assist them, either a close or distant relative or a social worker. The Swedish law, however, is hardly recent, and it was much criticized some years ago as being clearly discriminatory. Actually, under the term *single-parent family* there is no intended reference to illegitimacy, but rather the aloneness of an individual, man or woman, widowed, divorced or separated, who is faced with the upbringing of one or more children. And so, in the Quebec of today, the following fundamental question may well be asked concerning all the traditional forms of approach toward the family: Must a couple or an individual really be married to be able to assure a child the environment and care necessary for his or her maximum development? The answer to this question does not vary according to clear norms, but according to the cases involved, and it is for this reason that I shall try, in this book, to limit myself to a target group. What characterized this group is not the unity of the family structures, but a single common denominator that can best be described as instability: emotional instability, an unstable way of life, unstable adult relationships, and unstable socioeconomic circumstances.

In short, I believe that the prevention of deprived childhood will never be regulated by legislation or an official system of treatment, and that to exercise it effectively, direct aid must be given to certain groups of parents by assigning them guardians and offering them socioeducational treatment. The plan of this entire study is based on this fundamental assumption.

Thus chapter 1 deals with the present legislation and its application, pointing out the reforms made in the new Quebec act for the protection of minors. Will these reforms make possible the organization of valid and effective prevention? I do not think so, for the good reason that the laws permit intervention at the moment of crisis, but not prior to it.

Since it is impossible to show the effects of the recent legislation, I deal in chapter 2 with the effects of the past laws on child labor, as well as with the actual protection of children's rights through judicial and social interventions on their behalf. In short, I try to show that minors who do not have a family with the capacity or the willingness to look after them have always been the victims of society as well as its "aggressors" as juvenile delinquents.

Finally, chapter 3 is devoted to the study of a sample of parents selected among common-law prisoners. I thus describe a group whose living habits are relatively homogeneous, and I try to show what I mean by the term *target population*—those families where prevention can be considered an absolute necessity.

My findings are the result of research made possible by a grant of $3,000 from the Richelieu Foundation. The study was made on the basis of a questionnaire and interviews with the mothers and fathers of prisoners and their husbands and wives who are trying to keep the families of prisoners together and ensure the upbringing of the children. A young lawyer, Michéle Rouillard, met with most of these men and women, and I wish here to point out her contribution, particularly her intelligent and conscientious work, as well as her constant effort to understand the day-by-day dramas in the lives of these families, dramas that can very possibly weigh heavily on the future of their children.

In the conclusion to the book I comment on the rights that should be accorded children by our community and the protection we should guarantee them by assisting and educating their families. This approach is certainly not new, nor is it out of the ordinary, but it seems to have ramifications that are more and more important.

I have always believed, and this is true for most of the Western countries, that the intervention of the welfare state could mitigate the majority of our present social problems, or even cause them to disappear. However, the problems and the injustices minors are experiencing in the name of principles considered immutable, both in law and in fact, show the urgent need for us to agree that, in certain cases, the interests of the children can be more important than those of their parents. It is no longer a question of simply helping the family, but of reconsidering the true significance of this word in terms of the most favorable environment for the children and the defence of their rights.

Notes

1. For details, see S.R.Q. 1909, art. 7257; S.R.Q. 1925, chap. 194, art. 2; S.R.Q. 1941, chap. 325, art. 12.

2. The concept of forfeiture of parents' rights was introduced, however, in the civil code in 1977, in articles 245e and h.

3. H. Laborit, *L'Éloge de la Fuite* (Paris: Robert Laffont, 1976).

4. Ibid.

**Parenting and
Delinquent Youth**

1 Legal and Social Intervention

In Canada, minors come under two separate jurisdictions, one federal and the other provincial. The British North America Act gives the federal Parliament exclusive authority in matters of criminal law, which means that only Parliament can declare a given type of conduct criminal.

The legislatures of the ten provinces, however, have exclusive authority in the matter of justice administration within their respective territories, and they can authorize criminal sanctions in enforcing the laws that come under their constitutional jurisdiction. These concern infractions which theoretically are minor offences, but which in fact can be applied to certain behavior already defined as delinquent by the criminal code.

With regard to juvenile delinquency, the Juvenile Delinquents Act gives a standard definition for the whole of Canada, with the exception of the province of Newfoundland. This act, however, also covers all conduct defined as criminal under the provincial legislation and municipal regulations, and these vary.

However, the clauses relating to the protection of minors and juveniles change from one province to the other, for the latter have exclusive authority in this matter. This is even more significant in that juvenile court judges, at their own discretion, can hear the case before them under the Juvenile Delinquents Act or the Act for the Protection of Minors and Youth. The judge's decision does not necessarily depend on the nature of the offence, but may be influenced by the age and personality of the adolescent or child and the type of environment in which he has been raised.

Historically, the institution of two types of legislation applying to minors dates back to 1893. It was at this time that the Parliament of Ontario adopted the Youth Protection Act, which provided special measures for people violating the provincial laws. However, since this act did not cover cases of behavior defined as criminal by the code, in 1894, the Canadian Parliament voted in a law concerning the arrest, trial, and imprisonment of juvenile delinquents (Vict. 57-58, c. 58), amended in 1908 to become the Juvenile Delinquents Act and revised again in 1929.

Today, a project for the complete remodeling of this law is under study, and we seem to be oriented toward a revision of the whole concept of guilt where minors are concerned, as well as toward the protection of their rights before the court, where in the future their defense would be assured by a lawyer, as it is for adults. Since consultations between the provinces and the federal government are still going on, these reforms have not yet been ratified by the federal Parliament, and it is difficult to say when they will be voted on.

Standardization of the provincial legislation also is being proposed. As it is now, the age of criminal responsibility varies. In British Columbia, Manitoba, Alberta, and Quebec, it is eighteen; in Saskatchewan, Ontario, New Brunswick, Nova Scotia, and Prince Edward Island, it is sixteen; and in Newfoundland, it is seventeen. It is a matter of establishing the age of criminal majority at the same level as that of legal majority, which is eighteen years of age, and at the same time recognizing that the criminal code can apply only to delinquents of more than twelve or fourteen years, the others having to be heard under the provincial laws.

Concerning application of the law, all the provinces have created courts for minors called family courts or juvenile courts. These courts hear the cases concerning minors and the adults involved, and in certain provinces, Ontario, for example, separation cases are heard. Divorce, however, comes under a different jurisdiction.

For adults, the power of the juvenile court is limited to a maximum conviction of two years' imprisonment, but the judge can impose a concurrent penalty or refer the case to another court. Where minors are concerned, the juvenile judge can send those over fourteen years of age before the regular courts, but only in specific cases where there is an indictable offence. In practice, judges rarely use this measure, most of the time only in the case of recidivists.

According to the measures provided, the juvenile judge can order unconditional release, adjournment of the case for either a set or undetermined period, the imposition of a fine, reimbursement of damages or restitution, the appointment of a supervisor to assist the minor while living with his family, in a foster home or training center, or placement in an institution for a period of not more than 2 years.

The provinces are responsible for the organization of all services for the treatment of minors. These come under the jurisdiction of either the Department of Justice or the Department of Social Affairs. These services include receiving centers, clinics, where minors are examined and evaluated when so ordered by the judge, and schools of protection. The provincial governments directly or indirectly subsidize the public and private agencies that look after the placement of minors, adoptions, and children's aid in general.

The personnel of the children's services include probation officers attached to the juvenile courts and under the jurisdiction of the provincial Departments of Justice or Social Affairs. The training schools and training centers are under the direction of educators; these, like the social workers in child protection commissions and other extrajudicial services, are administratively responsible to the Department of Social Affairs. It is within this general context that measures are available to the province for the institutional or noninstitutional placement of minors.

Evolution of the Legislation Concerning Children

Where Quebec is concerned, the legislative framework includes specific laws dealing with juveniles and the family, among them

The Youth Protection Act (L.Q. 1977, c. 20).

An act respecting the protection of children subject to ill-treatment (L.Q. 1974, c. 59).

The Public Health Protection Act (L.Q. 1972, c. 42).

The Adoption Act (S.R.Q. 1964, c. 218).

An act respecting free education and compulsory school attendance (J-10 Eliz. II, c. 29; now Education Act, R.S.Q. 1964, c. 235, S. 272).

The Civil Code (legislation concerning the family).[1]

The Divorce Act (S.R.C. 1970, c. D-8).

It must be pointed out from the start that in the Canadian Code, the rights of parents are unconditional. Although the withdrawal of these rights is not provided for in the criminal code, the judge can pass sentence to have the child removed from the influence of his father, his mother, or both parents. The enforcement of such a measure obviously creates serious human problems, and it is generally used only in extreme cases. The placement of a child usually involves the agreement of his parents, and this can be obtained through the Commission for the Protection of Youth, the director of youth protection at a social service center, or a judge.

When it is a question of legal protection, it is the juvenile judge who is called upon to make the final decision and to intervene in all cases of litigation. This means that if the parents do not agree with the social worker on the measure proposed in the interest of the child, the juvenile court hears both parties and makes the decision. In the absence of parents or a guardian, the decision is also up to the judge.

An important fact to note is that according to the Youth Protection Act passed in 1978, the child must be informed, and if he is old enough, he must be consulted. This means that even if the parents agree to place their child, the latter can ask for the judge's intervention to prevent execution of the measure.

Regarding the sanction of the law, the judge who decides to place a juvenile delinquent in an institution also must inform him of the decision and explain the reason for his choice of this measure. On the whole, the Youth Protection Act ensures both social and legal protection.

As was mentioned earlier, the juvenile judge can apply this act to minors found guilty of an offence if he considers it preferable in the interest of the child to using an article in the Juvenile Delinquents Act. The preamble to the new Youth Protection Act is very explicit in this regard, for it states, "The Youth Protection Act is essentially to assure the protection, the reinsertion in his family and community, of every child whose security or development is threatened or who has committed an infraction of the law or of a regulation in force in Quebec" [free translation].

A commission for the protection of youth, composed of fourteen members, is charged with the task of seeing that the "rights of the child are respected and of undertaking the general supervision of the application of the Act [free translation]. The act contains eight chapters; the first is devoted to defining the functions of those responsible, such as the directors of youth protection in the social service centers, but also to designating the tasks of the various placement centers. The second chapter deals with children's rights, that of being informed and consulted, the ability to call upon the services of a lawyer, and the right never to be housed in a detention institution for adults or a police station. The third chapter describes how the members of the Youth Protection Commission are appointed, how they should sit, and the functions and duties they should assume.

The Powers of the Directors of Social Services

The second section of this chapter is devoted to a description of the responsibilities of the Director of Youth Protection. On the one hand, he must see to the tracking down of cases of children whose futures are in danger, take emergency measures, and ensure their execution. On the other hand, he is responsible for supervising the carrying out of measures ordered by the court.

Thus he has a double role, for he can take the initiative in intervening, always trying, however, "as far as possible to obtain the approval of the child's parents," but he also has to see that judicial decisions are obeyed.

Chapter 4 of the act is devoted to a description of the conditions justifying social intervention. I think it is worthwhile to cite them here in order to more clearly describe the framework of social protection. Measures are taken by the directors when:

1. The child's parents are no longer living, are neglecting him or trying to get rid of him, and there is no one else looking after him;
2. His mental, emotional, or physical development is endangered either because of loneliness or due to a lack of proper care;
3. He is deprived of the material conditions appropriate to his needs and to his family's resources;
4. He is being looked after by a person whose conduct or way of life threatens to place him in moral or physical danger;

5. He is of school age and does not attend school or is often absent without reason;
6. He is the victim of sexual abuse or is being physically maltreated as a result of intemperance or neglect;
7. He shows serious behavior problems;
8. He is forced or induced to beg, to work beyond his strength, or to perform in public in a manner unacceptable for his age;
9. He leaves a receiving center, a foster home, or his own home without authorization [free translation].

In article 40, the act also stipulates that "if a person has reasonable grounds to believe that a child has committed an infraction against a law or regulation in force in Quebec, the director must be informed of the case before legal action is taken [free translation]." The director can take the following measures:

1. Remove the child immediately from wherever he is living;
2. Place the child without delay in a receiving center, with a foster family, in a hospital, or appropriate agency;
3. Have a child of fourteen or more placed in preventive detention if he has reasonable grounds to believe that the child has committed an infraction against a Quebec law or regulation, and that this placement is necessary in view of the fact that the child constitutes a danger, or that there is every reason to presume that he will try to elude the application of the Act [free translation].

Voluntary Measures and the Discretionary Powers of Judges

Over and above these control measures, the director can recommend the voluntary measures defined in article 54, the supervision, placement, treatment, and training of the child. If the parents do not agree to these voluntary measures, the director, together with a person appointed by the Minister of Justice, can take the case to court as an emergency measure. When the court orders compulsory placement, the director is charged with deciding where the child should be placed and seeing that the conditions are adequate for his or her needs.

Finally, the director can submit a request to the Superior Court to be appointed guardian of a child who is abandoned, orphaned, neglected, or whose parents are not fulfilling their obligations and who in all probability will not be able to return to his or her family. As can be seen, the Director of Youth Protection has very extensive powers, and in the case of emergency measures, he has complete latitude, even if the parents refuse to give their consent. In this regard, the Quebec legislature has sought to protect children by challenging parents' rights if necessary. This aspect of the recent law of 1977 is important, for in the preceding legislation concerning youth protection, the powers of the social services were much more limited.

Chapter 5 of the act is devoted to actual legal intervention. Article 74 states that "only in the cases of emergency provided for in article 47 can the court hear the case of a child whose safety or development is threatened or who has been charged with a violation of a Quebec law or regulation, and then only when the case has been referred by the director together with a person appointed by the Minister of Justice, by the Commission or by an arbitrator whom he appoints . . ." or again, by the child or his parents, if they do not agree with:

1. A joint decision of the director and a person appointed by the Minister of Justice or a decision of the arbitrator named by the Commission . . .
2. The decision to prolong the duration of the voluntary placement in a receiving center [free translation].

Furthermore, although the abrogation of parents' rights is not specified in the legislation itself, article 91 stipulates in paragraph b that the judge can "deprive the parents of the exercise of certain rights of parental authority [free translation]."

In other words, the social services are asked to promote the agreement and collaboration of the family, and it is the court that must settle the matter in cases of conflict. However, according to article 101, the child, his parents, the director, the Commission, or the Attorney General can appeal the case before a superior court.

Chapters 6 and 7 of the act deal with the regulations concerning adults and the infractions of which adults can be guilty, as well as the penalties they can be subject to. Chapter 8 concerns temporary provisions and specifies in article 140 that the Juvenile Court is competent to hear:

1. Cases of young offenders under the Juvenile Delinquents Act (Revised Statutes of Canada, 1970, chapter J-3);
2. Cases of adoption under the Adoption Act (1969, chapter 64);
3. Cases of infractions against a Quebec law or regulation;
4. Other cases which are heard under the Youth Protection Act [free translation].

Article 151 states, furthermore, that adoption is possible "when the superior court has decreed the total abrogation of the parental authority of the mother and father [free translation]." This measure makes it possible to facilitate the adoption of children whose parents are living but incapable of fulfilling their obligations. The philosophy behind this measure is relatively new, considering the traditional view adopted in Canadian Legislation, where the rights of parents and their authority had priority, as it were, over the rights of the children.

In this regard, the act concerning the protection of ill-treated children, ratified on December 28, 1974, was an important innovation in Canadian legislative thinking. It established a committee which, upon complaint of a third party or in view of any other indication, can intervene on behalf of children subjected to maltreatment and victims of cruelty or negligence on the part of their parents or other people responsible for their care.

The committee has the power to make an investigation and present recommendations either to the court or to the minister involved in the administration of the Youth Protection Act. The minister can and should respect the anonymity of the people reporting the facts about the maltreatment of children—an important innovation. In the past, neighbors or other members of the family hesitated to appear as witnesses before the courts against cruel or negligent parents, not wanting to be directly involved in the case. Health services personnel, and especially doctors, had a great deal of difficulty giving evidence before juvenile judges regarding the origin of the injuries to babies or young children they were called upon to treat.

The committee relieves the medical profession of having to submit proof before the law, for it makes the investigation and presents reports to confirm or negate the diagnoses established in the hospitals. It may be said, nonetheless, that intervention of this kind is always dependent on prior observation.

Doctors who deliver the baby of a woman who is mentally ill avoid making a prognosis, even if there is strong reason to believe that the natural mother may subject her baby to cruelty or harm it in some way and, in any case, in her state of mental health, not be able to assume the upbringing of the child. There must be proof of cruelty, proof of blows or other signs, for the practitioner to agree to designate it as such.

It may be claimed, then, that despite the very interesting legislative reforms in Quebec and elsewhere, the child is always the victim of the greatest hazard of all—birth itself. This is not due to the inability of the legislators to assure children full and complete protection; it is much more the refusal of the community to intervene within the confines of its basic component—the family.

In both the case of the child in need of protection and the juvenile delinquent, society reacts only when there is a crisis situation. Contrary to the assistance that can be given an adult, the majority of measures taken on behalf of children involve taking them partially or completely in charge, the establishment or reconstruction of a living environment, and always the use of some form of pressure and control. The adult can receive financial aid; the child and adolescent require a proper environment and education, and these entail much higher costs and a social investment whose results are much more problematic.

In effect, it is hard enough to foresee the results of a child's development in the context of a family considered to have a positive influence, but it is practically impossible to make any valid scientific evaluations of a child's ability to readapt once he has gone through experiences much too difficult for his age. In concrete terms, the means at society's disposal are

1. Assistance to the family.
2. Assistance given the child by a social worker.
3. Temporary or permanent placement of the child in a home other than that of his or her parents.
4. Placement of the child in a special institution.

Social workers must obtain the consent of the parents to proceed with one or several of these measures. In Quebec, these measures come under the jurisdiction of the social service centers (SSC) created under the Youth Protection Act, ratified by the Quebec National Assembly, December 19, 1977. As mentioned before, the directors of youth protection in the social service centers can take emergency measures in cases where the parents are opposed to the application of their decision. However, it is up to the juvenile court judge to give the final verdict on the treatment to be given the child.

With regard to juvenile delinquents, judges can impose measures similar to those provided for children in need of protection, but the aid, assistance, or supervision will be given not by a social service center, but by a probation officer. The probation services for minors, however, are integrated in the social service centers, and the academic training of their personnel differs very little from that required for social workers. In addition, magistrates have certain means at their disposal, educative or punitive, depending on the approach adopted toward juvenile delinquency as such.

Judicial decisions include the following sentences:

1. Reprimand
2. Supervision of the court
3. Fine or restitution
4. Temporary or prolonged placement in a training school and receiving center
5. Deferment of punishment
6. Referral to another court
7. Others

Contrary to the justice system for adults, decisions for minors have various designations, and it is important to specify what these terms mean, for they vary according to those who use them—jurists, criminologists, social workers, and, of course, specialists, such as psychologists and psychiatrists. Thus the reprimand may appear in the statistics under the heading "adjournment of the case sine die." The judge sees the child, his family, or whoever is in charge of him and decides to maintain the status quo. He asks the minor to change his behavior and lets him return to his home without setting the date for further appearance before the court.

The term *supervision of the court* also can be called *placement on probation*. The judge expressly entrusts the child to his parents, one of his parents, a third party, or a probation officer, while authorizing him to live at home. *Supervision of the court* also can be accompanied by *placement* in a foster home, a training center, or a home caring for a group of children for a short or indefinite period. A *fine* or *restitution* of stolen goods is imposed on the parents or on the minor if he is able to work in order to pay the victim damages or pay the fine. *Placement in a training school* generally does not extend beyond a period of 2 years. *Deferment of punishment* means that the judge warns the minor that if he recidivates, he will be sent to a training school or placed in detention, or the judge agrees to free the child under certain conditions, provided that he report to a probation officer and appear before the magistrate on a set date or one to be determined. Minors who are sent before a different court are also designated as being *referred* to a court of sessions. Among the other measures, there is *placement in a hospital for the mentally ill* and *incarceration.*

Besides the terms describing the various judicial decisions, there is a description of the services. Here again, the treatment of minors differs from that of adults, since there is no question of isolation, that is, prison. It should be noted also that contrary to the delinquent adult, protection of the child or adolescent is urgent, so that the delays in education and training—delays that are of the utmost importance considering the rapid evolution of other children of the same age—can be compensated for or overcome.

In practice, however, this compensation is possible in only a very small percentage of cases. There are two reasons for this. First, the fact that in our system there are two superimposed types of intervention, social and judicial, necessarily retards decision making. The social services require a more or less prolonged period in order to try to find solutions in collaboration with the family. When they do not succeed in settling a case, they call on the judge. The juvenile judge, for his part, also must have a certain length of time to obtain an evaluation and a presentence report, usually prepared by a probation officer. Furthermore, when he makes his decision, he always has to take into account the resources available to him.

Actually, the judge's sentence cannot always be enforced. This means that the judge may consider that the minor should be placed in a given institution and order that this be done, but the selection committee of the institution concerned has the power to refuse the case, under the pretext that its program would not be suitable.

Institutional Treatment

In the past, the institutional resources of Quebec included protection schools and training centers. Since 1971, however, by virtue of the Health and Social Services Act (L.Q. 1971, chap. 48), all these institutions are called by the same name of training centers. Within this framework, distinctions have been made, defining the objectives of these centers according to four categories: emergency, transition, observation, and preventive or punitive detention. Since all these types of institutions do not exist throughout the entire territory, in practice there is always some confusion between the theoretical definitions of their tasks and the reality. Even more, given the needs of the clientele, it is obvious that it would be impossible to mathematically determine whether a child needed emergency measures with or without observation, or if he or she should go to a transition center after having been in a detention center.

At the time that a distinction was made between the protection schools and receiving centers, also defined in the Juvenile Delinquents Act as reform schools, children frequently had to wait for their admission to one or the other until space was available. The main difference in the systems was that the schools gave academic courses or taught a trade, awarding diplomas valid on the labor market. In this sense, the period of waiting was a waste of time. However, since the results of teaching this category of pupil has always been problematic, to say the least, it is very difficult to assess the setback caused by this waiting period. Today all receiving centers provide some education, within or outside their services.

According to the survey done in 1975 by the Youth Protection Committee, the statistics show seventy institutions with room for 6,000 clients, and a personnel of 3,500 employees. In 1975, there were 4,958 minors under eighteen years of age in these institutions, and the annual cost of treatment per child amounted to $10,000.

Given the tremendous sums involved, and that the results obtained through institutional placement, both in terms of academic or professional training and rehabilitation, are rather disappointing, it is not very likely that there will be any spectacular development of the system over the next few years.

During their survey, the commissioners found that the children could neither read nor write after a prolonged stay in an institution with school facilities, if only at the elementary level, and considering the programs and the means of putting them into practice, there is little chance that this can change. In this regard, it is important to note that contrary to the methods used in the past, where the religious educators imposed their teaching, today's educators, secular and unionized, are content to recommend it. Lacking motivation, such an approach is suitable for only a very limited number of pupils, either very exceptional juvenile delinquents or particularly gifted people who under any circumstances develop and progress, even if all those around them continue to fall behind.

It may be pointed out that regression of pupils in the specialized institutional system is not peculiar to Quebec. It is a general trend, related in part to the lowering of educational standards in all the schools, but above all to the constant use of experimental methods of treatment that are often abandoned before the personnel can learn and use them.[2]

Individual Treatment

Over and above institutional placement, there is individual placement in foster homes. The people involved are substantially the same, for children in need of protection, as well as juvenile delinquents, can be sent to a center or a foster family or be transferred from one to the other.

Since I believe that foster homes will be used more and more in the future as a means of placement, I wish to give them particular attention. The administrative authorities seem to be aware of the importance of this community resource, for the scale of remuneration has been raised after a long period when the rates maintained were sometimes below the actual cost of keeping a traumatized or problem child. These rates are now on a scale going from $4.50 to $7.50 a day, depending on the age of the child, with the possibility of additional adjustments amounting to a maximum of $10 for homes looking after several children. Supplements are provided for particularly difficult or handicapped children.

Exactly what is a foster home? In order to answer this question, in 1976 I did a study in Montreal and in a region of Paris.[3] In my report of some three hundred pages, I tried to answer the following questions:

1. What type of children are placed in foster families by the social services and the courts?
2. What are the characteristics of foster parents?
3. What are the present trends concerning this form of placement?
4. What reforms seem to be needed to correct the negative results we find today regarding this type of placement?

I continue here with the same type of analysis of foster families, completing my basic research by examining the application of the most recent legislation concerning minors and marginal youths.

To begin with, a preliminary remark is in order: the concept itself of the foster family, contrary to that of the receiving center, is not new; it is its name that can be considered proper to our era and that has much more significance than one might at first think. In this regard, it could be said that the regulation passed in France 7 years after the revolution of 1789, that is, in 1796, still coincides with certain present-day realities. It reads:

Wet-nurses and other inhabitants of the countryside may keep the children entrusted to them up to the age of twelve years, on condition that they feed and lodge them suitably at a price and under conditions which will be determined . . . and that they send them to schools to receive the instruction given other children of the community and the canton [free translation].

What has changed fundamentally are the types of children placed and the types of foster families. Placement by private individuals has not disappeared, but it is not within my competence to discuss this. I would simply mention that it has become generalized, and that in every sector of the population we now find natural parents who are obliged, or decide, to place their children during the day, on weekends, or during the holidays with a foster family. In these cases, however, arrangements are made between the two families, which do not necessitate the intervention of the community as long as there is no evidence of abuse or exploitation.

However, placement of the child by the social services is governed by rules and clauses and entails many consequences justifying the intervention of social workers and judges. The children thus placed are either orphans, youngsters rejected by their parents, or uncontrollable, sick, or delinquent youths. They vary in age from several months to eighteen years. Generally, it is a question of minors who have had bad experiences, all the more traumatic since they were unable to understand and overcome them because of their tender age. Thus, according to the most recent statistics published by the Quebec Social Services, the largest number of such children are in the category of from five to eleven years old, as shown in table 1-1.

The data I obtained during my research on foster families in 1976 showed the same trend, which in itself is very significant. The fact is that there is no question of continuity, of establishing a link between the two families, that of the natural parents and that of the foster parents, in order for the child to get used to living in two milieus from the time he or she first becomes a foster child; there is a total rupture. The five-year-old category is very meaningful in this regard.

In effect, single mothers, unstable couples, and parents incapable of fulfilling their obligations generally manage to look after their very young babies. It is when they begin to move about, have contacts with the outside, and express themselves that the natural family decides to refuse the responsibility of their upbringing. The refusal generally occurs after a crisis or crises in which the child is the main victim, and such crises leave their mark.

When it comes to the intervention of a third party, the police, social workers, or a judge, an effort is made at first to keep the child with his natural family. Even in the case of parents who are cruel, negligent, irresponsible, or criminal, the present trend, at least in Quebec, but elsewhere too, is to try to restore the family unit by offering the adults support.

Table 1-1

Increase in the Number of Children Placed in Foster Homes in Quebec at the End of the Month, According to Age Group, Fiscal Year 1975-1976

Year/Month		0-4 yrs		5-11 yrs		Age Group 12-15 yrs		16-17 yrs		Total	
		Number	Percent	Number	Percent	Number	Percent	Number	Percent	Number	Percent
1975	April	1,513	7.4	8,116	40.0	6,837	33.6	3,864	19.0	20,330	100
	May	1,495		8,074		6,896		3,952		20,417	
	June	1,456	7.2	7,887	39.2	6,814	34.0	3,950	19.6	20,107	100
	July	1,452		7,689		6,779		3,787		19,707	
	August	1,418		7,416		6,676		3,699		19,209	
	September	1,421	7.3	7,476	38.7	6,776	35.0	3,666	19.0	19,339	100
	October	1,391		7,481		6,838		3,689		19,399	
	November	1,395		7,466		6,849		3,789		19,508	
	December	1,396	7.1	7,392	37.5	6,910	35.0	4,017	20.4	19,715	100
1976	January	1,359		7,325		6,885		4,074		19,643	
	February	1,369		7,310		6,848		4,208		19,735	
	March	1,399	7.0	7,308	36.6	6,935	34.7	4,328	21.7	19,970	100

Source: *Report of the Department of Social Affairs of Quebec.*

This approach is justified by the old principle that "bad parents are better than no parents at all," but also by the tremendous responsibility the community assumes when it removes a child from its natural milieu. No one can guarantee that the child will become acclimatized to a foster family and that the latter will be able to fully answer his or her needs.

However, a number of studies have shown the catastrophic effects of numerous placements, the victims being children who adapt badly in the families to which they are entrusted. The hazard of birth is not the community's responsibility, but that of a voluntary placement, decided jointly by the natural parents and social workers, or a placement ordered by the juvenile judge entails a decision all the more difficult to evaluate in that its consequences cannot be foreseeable or measured beforehand. In short, it is not surprising that the social services and those of the courts hesitate before placing a child outside his or her home and try first to solve the problem within the natural family.

Then, too, the detecting of disadvantaged children or young delinquents—and for those under twelve years of age there is some confusion between the two, if not in law, at least in fact—is very difficult and rather slow. In this regard, when we talk of prevention, in my opinion, we are expressing a fond hope. Not only do we not prevent childhood traumas, we still wait until they become irreversible before taking actual measures through social intervention. Out of respect for the rights of parents and the inviolability of a person's private life, verifications and controls are nonexistent. It is surprising that although in the Western countries women give birth in the hospitals nowadays, doctors intervene only in the most extreme cases to ask the court to have the baby immediately removed from its family milieu, even when they know that the mother is suffering from a psychic illness that makes her incapable of assuming her responsibilities. This reluctance to intervene that is seen everywhere and is furthermore encouraged by laws and regulations makes true prevention impossible. The community intervenes when the child's situation demands it and does so at a pace governed by administrative constraints and not by the needs of the child, however obvious they may be.

What are the results of this manner of proceeding? During my research, I systematically asked foster parents questions about the state of the child when they received her or him. They all replied that generally the child could not be considered normal or good, either physically or from the point of view of cultural development, learning experience, or schooling. In my research, I was interested, of course, only in children placed in foster homes because of the inability or refusal of their natural parents to look after them, not for reasons of infirmity or sickness.

To conclude my remarks on the characteristics of children placed in foster homes, I believe it possible to state that they are children who have experienced trauma too serious for their age and their ability to understand, children who have psychosomatic problems and who consequently all have much more difficulty in adjusting than the average child who has received all the attention required in infancy.

Characteristics of Foster Parents

Who are the kind of people willing to accept the risk of taking care of children who have been mistreated or delinquent? This is a very important question, for in order to develop this form of community placement, it is necessary to make a prior study of the characteristics and motivations of foster parents.

First of all, contrary to educators and the personnel of the social services, foster parents are people who are not, and cannot be, unionized. The basic rate of remuneration since 1978 is $2,000 a year in round figures. This is not really remuneration, however, but rather reimbursement of the costs involved. There is no salary, then, for foster parents looking after only one child, while in homes that take several youngsters, for the number of hours devoted to them, compensation is minimal.

It therefore seems to me that our approach to foster families should be on a different level from that based on a time/payment analysis. With regard to motivation, foster parents are divided into two groups. The first group is composed of people who would like to adopt a child, but because of the norms, legislation, and delays involved, decide in the meantime to take a minor referred by a judge. The social workers warn them in vain that they will not be able to keep the child, that she or he is the "property" of his natural parents, however cruel or preposterous they may be. Nevertheless, some of these people hope that the "little one" will get used to them and stay. In short, this is a form of disguised adoption, its success depending on the clear-sightedness of the social workers who make the placement, as well as the courage of the juvenile judge in eventually breaking the formal ties that bind the child to his or her natural parents, in the interest of the child.

The second group is composed of so-called middle-class families. They want to take in other people's children either to fill a void in their home or because the wife wants something to do without leaving the house. The only experience such a woman has is often that of mother, and she wants to give those entrusted to her the benefit. In these homes, older children, juvenile delinquents, and retarded, sick, or crippled children are accepted. Sometimes such a couple decides to take only one child; sometimes they reorganize their lifestyles completely in order to become a foster home, which may take in up to ten minors with diverse problems.

Most foster parents are men and women who come from large families. Childhood, in itself, is not a problem for them, but a natural fact of life that offers many compensations. Foster parents, incidentally, generally say they often have more trouble with the natural parents than with the children entrusted to their care.

First of all, there is a basic conflict in most cases between the natural mother and the foster mother. When visits and contacts are allowed, this conflict inevitably affects the child. Involved here is a typical case of jealousy. The natural mother, who has not been able to control her child or look after him or her properly, cannot forgive the foster mother for succeeding where she has failed. It is an emotional conflict in which the child becomes the prize in a competition between two adult females. Faced with the mother's sudden changes of mood, periods of indifference alternating with demonstrations of affection, the foster mother feels deprived. After all, she is the one who looks after the child, while the visiting mother takes advantage of weekly outings to "spoil her little one" as she pleases. Torn between the two women, the child is unable to adjust, but no judge can sever the relationship and refuse the natural parents their rights as long as they have not been legally forfeited.

I may add that in Quebec, where there is no abrogation of parents rights provided in the criminal code, the procedure is complicated and difficult. In practice, visiting rights are rarely refused, and even in these exceptional cases, it has never been possible to put the measure into effect. Thus foster parents must face the hostility and threats of the natural parents who want to regain the affection of their child without making the effort this involves. These basic truths are well known to social workers and juvenile judges, but nothing can be done without challenging the rights of the natural parents.

Also, when asking foster parents to take children who a priori can be described as difficult, as compared with those growing up in a normal way, the administrative and judicial services warn them that they must never look upon them as their own children. However, as psychiatrists and psychologists well know, one cannot look after a child or an adolescent without becoming emotionally attached. There is a basic contradiction, then, and a sort of hypocrisy underlying the very measure of placement in a foster home.

In an institution, educators can more easily avoid the development of emotional ties with individual pupils; in a foster home, this would seem practically impossible, except in those which take in several minors who constitute small groups, often highly unstable because of frequent changes from place to place.

What is the attitude of the sociolegal services toward foster homes? This question is complex. First of all, in Quebec, a distinction must be made between three categories of foster homes, excluding those which are adoption homes in fact, if not in legal terms. The first group includes homes attached to an institution. These people take children referred by training schools or receiving centers and can avail themselves of the advice and technical support of the institutional personnel; but above all, they have the possibility of quickly sending back a child they cannot control and taking him or her back after the educators have succeeded in placating the youngster.

The second group includes homes that take a child referred by social workers following a voluntary agreement on the part of the natural parents or on order of the court. Foster parents of this type generally have little contact with the administrative authorities if the placement proves successful; if not, they prefer not to renew the experience.

The third group includes all those who take care of several children. These serve as emergency homes, transitional placements, or ones that may sometimes be prolonged, but are often of an uncertain duration. It is in this category of home that the instability of the child's situation creates the most negative effects.

The fact is, however, that it is just these very homes which, for the administrative services, chronically overwhelmed with requests and unable to find the proper environment in the institutions, become an important placement resource. In effect, the institutions prove insufficient to answer the demand, and in view of the autonomy of the institutions and the dearth of space, foster homes remain a solution for the immediate future as well as over the long term. We might add that there is no reason for this to change. According to the report of the Batshaw Committee in 1976, the annual cost of keeping a minor in a training center is $10,000, while that of a foster home is generally not more than $2,000. It can be easily understood why the state does not wish to increase the number of places available, which can now accommodate about 5,000 youths.

To put it bluntly, the question is: Should a foster family provide a home or an emergency measure for the administrative authorities? Have the failures related to frequent moves of certain children from one foster home to another been due to the inability of the foster parents to bring their charges up properly or to the way this community resource is used?

It must be admitted that training schools and receiving centers are in a position to defend themselves against sociolegal pressures, regardless of regulations and selection boards, whereas foster parents are individuals belonging to a family unit and have difficulty joining with others and forming a common front. In other words, foster families are practically helpless against the constraints of the administration.

For example, let us say that for certain foster mothers, not to accept a temporary placement is to risk having a child they have been looking after for some time taken from them. True or false, these fears exist and make relations with the administrative authorities particularly difficult, since foster families have no official or other defender, such as an administration board or a union capable of calling a strike.

According to the reports of the Quebec Department of Social Affairs, the number of placements in foster homes are becoming fewer, as can be seen in table 1-2. It is practically impossible, however, to comment on these changes without taking three main factors into consideration: the lower birth rate (very sudden in Quebec), the relatively fewer sociolegal decisions involving the placement of children outside their natural families, and finally, if not above all, the diminution of the number of parents wanting to take in children and play the role of foster family.

Table 1-2
Placements in Foster Homes

Year	Number
1960	7,026
1969	31,115
1972	26,790
1975-1976	19,760

Note: These are the last statistics available. We choose the years given because of the large drop in the figures. In this regard, it should be noted that for 1960, the number of foster homes does not indicate the true situation. At this time, these homes were dependent on the institutions and private agencies, and the data were incomplete. It was only in 1969 that the social services, set up and reorganized under the direct authority of the department, carried out a survey of all the foster homes available.

In this regard, account also must be taken of the factors affecting foster parents as well as other couples: the amendment of the legislation concerning divorce, which resulted in marriages becoming more unstable, the professionalization of married women, and the increased percentage of women wanting to work outside the home and now able to do so.

What, then, are the future prospects? First of all, I should mention that in the new Youth Protection Act, the legislator explicitly recognizes the child's right to be consulted about the measures that should be taken on his behalf. This means that from now on a child will be able to oppose his natural parents' wish to take him back and say that he prefers to remain in the foster home in which he has been placed, or on the contrary, that he wants to stay in his own home, even if it is considered an improper environment for his upbringing.

In the second place, the social services, and especially their directors, have been given broader powers. They are now obliged to see that voluntary measures, decided on together with the parents, are carried out as well as those ordered by the juvenile judge. This means that the directors of the social services will inevitably be led to look for placement possibilities other than institutional ones, for it is highly unlikely that the authorities will decide to increase the available accommodations in the institutions. In this regard, I would point out that in their conclusions, the commissioners charged with the survey of training centers in Quebec wrote the following:

It is astonishing to see youngsters of fifteen who, after a prolonged stay in an institution, can neither read, write nor do arithmetic.

In addition, we find a profusion of treatment methods, a sort of technical and scientific inflation where, in their desire for innovation, however laudable, each practitioner is trying the latest methods without having the time to evaluate them [free translation].

At the same time, it seems that homes that take charge of a number of children will be in a better position to demand that set working conditions and remuneration be stipulated, and that in certain respects they be more in keeping with those which prevail in other sectors. Thus we can envision, as in France, guaranteeing foster mothers a minimum salary and the same fringe benefits that exist for other categories of workers, such as the right to vacations, retirement pensions, sick leaves, and some form of employment security.

One thing is certain, and this is that foster families fulfill an important social role in replacing the natural family for children or delinquents in need of care. Given the ever-increasing costs of institutional treatment for children, the foster family offers far too many advantages for us not to try to organize this resource within the community. We must make a special effort to do away with the present instability that occurs in noninstitutional placement, for in my opinion, it is not inherent in its form, but is due much more to the regulations and methods that govern this measure for child protection.

If we agree, however, that this social resource must be developed, there is an urgent need to set up norms much more specific than they have been in the past on which to base the decisions concerning such matters as

1. The choice of foster families to be recruited
2. Their professional status in the community
3. The remuneration and social benefits of the foster mother
4. The responsibilities and official commitments of foster parents with regard to the duration of the child's placement

Where recruiting is concerned, there is no absolute model of what could be defined as good parents. The proof of excellence appears only many years later, that is, too late, when the child has already reached adulthood. It is always a case of putting one's trust in the couples who ask to be given a child, of reserving the right to observe the child, but also of acknowledging the duty of the social services to keep informed and give the necessary medical and educational support.

However, as difficult as it is at the present time to fulfill specific requirements concerning foster parents, especially where duration of placement is concerned, increased remuneration and a recognition of the professional status of the foster mother must be accompanied by certain restrictions. It is inconceivable that a child be buffeted from one home to another. It is inhuman and shocking to come across adolescents who have been ejected from perhaps thirty foster homes over a period of 1 or 2 years. It is also inhuman to allow a couple to become attached to a child and live in constant fear of having to give it up with several hours' notice. In short, as long as foster parents were seen as answering needs denied by the natural parents, such situations could exist, but if we agree that they have become a social and community resource as homes for one or more children, we cannot continue the traditional approach.

Finally, the children to be placed in foster homes should be selected according to age and an evaluation of their particular characteristics. Obviously, a delinquent should not be referred to a home simply because there is no room for him in a receiving center and to avoid his going to prison. In other words, a minor should be placed with a foster family on the basis of an evaluation of the degree of deterioration his personality has suffered, his past history, and his motivations; the foster home should not be used by the socioadministrative system as a means of solving a case.

At present, the children placed in foster homes include newborn babies as well as adolescents who have committed serious crimes and are recidivists. One can easily understand, then, the problems that result, and especially the numerous changes from one home to another, which are extremely damaging to those concerned and in themselves a powerful force for marginal behavior. It is a proven fact that the child who feels constantly rejected ends up unable to adapt anywhere.

Notes

1. See also the project for the new civil code, which has not yet been adopted by the commission headed by Paul Crépeau.

2. This opinion is discussed by Maurice Cusson, one of the authors of the report of the commission to study the readaptation of children and adolescents placed in receiving centers. "Guide des centres d'accueil de transition et de réadaptation du Québec," vol. 1, Batshaw Commission, Department of Social Affairs, Communications Branch, January 1976.

3. A. Parizeau, "Le placement familial de l'enfance," unpublished report, Montreal, Quebec, 1976. Available at the Documentation Service of the ICCC, Université de Montréal.

4. Report of the Task Force on the Rehabilitation of Children and Adolescents Placed in Training Centers. Guide to the Training, Transition, and Rehabilitation Centers in Quebec, Volume I, the Batshaw Committee, Department of Social Affairs, Communications Center, January 1976.

2 Child Protection and Juvenile Delinquency

As shown in the preceding chapter, the Quebec legislature has tried to answer the present social needs of young people. In view of the changes in family life brought about by the evolution of society, it was deemed necessary to recognize the right of children to be informed and given the choice of where they want to live. From now on a child can state his preference between one or the other of his natural parents in cases of separation or divorce, or with regard to foster or adoptive parents. At the same time, for the first time in Canadian legislation, citizens are given the right to report cases of maltreatment of children without having to bear witness or divulge their identity.

Can these reforms be considered assurance of a true preventive policy? It is almost impossible to answer this question at this stage; the new protection act has only just been put into effect in Quebec. One thing is certain, however, and this is that where treatment of the family and minors is concerned, the legislation has infinitely less importance than the attitude of the community regarding the rights and obligations of young people. However regressive or progressive the sociojudicial legislation may be, it is useless if it does not correspond with the real needs of the people and groups concerned.

To illustrate these assertions, I shall try in this chapter to present a brief historical retrospective to complete the study of some statistical and judicial data. Where the legislation is concerned, there are disparities between the evolution of society and the principles set down in the criminal code. With regard to its application, one finds contradictions and constant gaps. Finally, as far as preventive policies for specific groups or areas goes, it seems that it has been impossible to arrive at an overall plan to date. The consequences of this are to be found in the case records.

Crime Legislation and the Evolution of Society

In Canada, the Juvenile Delinquents Act has not changed very much throughout the first half of the twentieth century, but the attitude toward minors, in fact the whole concept of adult authority, has changed very rapidly, giving rise to a great many pressures in the area of community intervention in the family. In Quebec in particular, up to World War II and even until the sixties, the ethical norms imposed by the community on the rising generation were stable, strict, and uniform. Nonconformity to one of these norms, as narrow

21

and ridiculous as it may have been objectively, was enough to be considered "headstrong," the "black sheep" of the family, or a "no good." In the family circle, as well as in the school, the child owed respect and obedience to adults, who, in principle, acted in his best interest.

Where work was concerned, for we must not forget that at the beginning of the century child labor was common in Quebec, both in the country and the city, the minor was obliged under threat of severe punishment, but not necessarily imposed by the courts, to conform to the wishes of the supervisors, for whom increased productivity was still the only thing that counted.

Depending on whether the child belonged to a family that had sufficient means to ensure his support or to one that obliged him to work, the youth was less or more exposed to run-ins with the police. The delinquents known to the courts, therefore, were generally abandoned children and those from disadvantaged areas. Because of the stock market crash, from 1929 to about 1939, the definition of the disadvantaged covered all the unemployed, who had only the right to rather uncertain direct help.

The "black sheep" of wealthy families or those with a stable, even if not very large, income found themselves in boarding schools administered by priests, where the system was stricter than that in the schools from which they had succeeded in having themselves expelled. I might add that the term *minor* included everyone under twenty-one, and for those under the age of majority, there were certain restraints then that do not exist today.

To be under twenty-one meant that one could not rent a room and did not have the right to be in the street after nightfall, to say nothing of such dissolute behavior as kissing a girl or boy in public. The written authorization of the father or guardian was required everywhere and for everyone and was accepted as an established fact. This authoritarianism caused some youngsters to react in personal revolt, which, mild as it may have been, automatically drew the fire of the law.

In this regard, the imprecision of article I, paragraph 2 of the Juvenile Delinquents Act, whose present form dates back to 1929, is a good illustration of the thinking of the time. It defines juvenile delinquency in the following terms:

> Juvenile delinquent means any child who violates any provision of the Criminal Code or of any federal or provincial statute, or of any by-law or ordinance of any municipality, or who is guilty of sexual immorality or any similar form of vice, or who is liable by reason of any other act to be committed to an industrial school or juvenile reformatory under any federal or provincial statute.

According to this legislation, applying, let us not forget, to all children of seven years "and even less," an adolescent appearing on a hot July day at the corner of Peel and St. Catherine Streets in a slightly transparent dress could very well have been declared a juvenile delinquent. It was up to the police to judge when such descriptions as "sexual immorality" or "any similar form of vice" were applicable, and they did so in accordance with the morals and customs of the time.

Like the police, employers also had the means to bring minors to their senses when they refused to serve as beasts of burden. The following is an extract from the report of the Royal Commission of Enquiry on Labor and Capital, which sat early in the century in the good old city of Montreal and heard the testimony of the young and not so young.

Q: You are a cigar worker?

A: Yes, sir,

Q: How old are you?

A: I was 14 last January 10th.

Q: In saying that you are a cigar maker, you mean to say that you have served your apprenticeship, don't you?

A: Yes, sir.

Q: For how long?

A: Three years.

Q: You started work at the age of 11?

A: Yes, sir.

Q: How many hours a day do you work?

A: Sometimes ten hours, other times, eight hours; it's whatever is wanted. . . .

Q: Why did you pay fines, do you remember?

A: Sometimes because there was too much talking; more often it was for that.

Q: You were never beaten?

A: Yes. Not so that I was injured, but it has happened to us, and sometimes we didn't cut the cigar casing properly and they would hit us on the head.

Q: Do they usually hit the children this way?

A: Often.

Q: Were you ever hit during the first year of your apprenticeship?

A: Yes, sir.

Q: Did you see other children beaten?

A: Yes. . . .

Q: Do you know of a factory that has a store-room?

A: Yes, sir.

Q: Did you ever see children put in this room?

A: Yes, sir.

Q: How old were the children?

A: I can't say how old.

Q: Younger than you?

A: No, sir.

Q: Why were they put in the store-room?
A: Because they were wasting time.
Q: Who put them there?
A: The man who was in charge of the press.
Q: Do you know whether this man wears a policeman's badge?
A: Yes, sir.
Q: Are the children afraid of him?
A: No.
Q: Were they handled roughly when in the store-room?
A: No, sir.
Q: How long did they generally stay there?
A: Until 7 o'clock.
G: When were they put there?
A: In the afternoon.
G: Was it till 7 o'clock in the evening, or for 7 hours?
A: 7 o'clock in the evening. They put them there in the afternoon until 7 o'clock in the evening.
Q: What time do the workers leave the factory?
A: Usually at five and sometimes six o'clock.
Q: Do you mean to say these children stayed in the store-room after the workers had left the factory?
A: Yes, sir.
Q: Who let them out: was it the person who put them there?
A: Yes, sir; I think so; I never saw him.
Q: Is the store-room heated?
A: I don't know.
Q: On what floor of the factory is this room located?
A: In the cellar.
Q: Is there a furnace in the cellar?
A: No, sir.
Q: Is there a window in the store-room?
A: No.
Q: When the children were there, did you never hear them call to be let out?
A: No, sir.
Q: At what age did you leave school?
A: Ten and a half.
Q: Do you know how to read and write?
A: A little.
Q: Do you know the four rules of arithmetic?
A: I don't know if I remember them.
Q: Are you an orphan?
A: No, sir.

Society has progressed a great deal since the time when the commissioners wondered why child workers who were locked up in the storeroom did not dare call for help, but not in terms of understanding children, only in terms of its socioeconomic structures.

Child labor is now forbidden, and generally speaking, the norms, rules, and limitations governing the conduct imposed on minors are no longer the same. A child who does not get along with his family can leave once he has reached the age of sixteen, and even before. Now he can find a livelihood; rent a room by himself, with someone else, or with several others, and not be in trouble with the law. Nowadays it is possible to leave school, return, and readjust. It is relatively easy to travel, to change one's environment, to rebel and even marry before anyone decides to exercise adult authority, which only serves to keep this rebellion alive.

By refusing to abandon its rights, the family in certain cases ceases to be the sole protective shield and even accepts the loss of all contact with the adolescent, hoping that he will come back sooner or later of his own accord. For example, in large cities, the police sometimes are obliged to take adolescents they arrest for petty infractions to training centers because they no longer live with their parents and have broken off all contact with them.

Criminologists and sociologists who have tried to describe this phenomenon abound, and few subjects have given rise to such an abundance of scientific study as juvenile delinquency and the evolution of its causes. Nevertheless, the Quebec situation has been analyzed less frequently than that of the United States, for example, where the number of publications on the subject is inordinate.

I do not believe, however, that we can benefit from all this collection of work to analyze the reactions of the Quebec community, for I am deeply convinced that in order to make generalizations and comparisons, we must first isolate the factors particular to the community under study. True, parent/ child relationships have dominant characteristics common to all contexts, but the social framework in which they exist influences and molds them. In western Europe, for example, the difficulty an adolescent has in earning enough money to live and getting authorization to rent an apartment or obtain medical care without the intervention of parents or guardians undoubtedly influences the maintenance of formal relationships, which is hardly the case in North America. The autonomy of minors vis-à-vis their family creates a direct pressure on the community regarding the young people, and this occasions some curious injustices. Thus it is that a young person who lives at home has less chance of obtaining a grant for his studies than one who has broken away and is "camping" with others in an apartment that he was able to rent in spite of his age of legal minority. By answering his needs, the community implicitly penalizes the families that assume those needs themselves.

The fact remains that in order to measure the influence of the resignation of the family, owing to the authority crisis, on the increase in juvenile delinquency coming before the courts, historical analyses are needed. Unfortunately, the documents are incomplete and the whole system of court statistics is such that it is almost impossible to go back in time. Even comparisons between the last few decades are difficult because of the lack of data, of factual and precise descriptions, and the fact that the court records on minors often do not include the motivation for the sentences. We shall therefore have to settle for some remarks based on the evidence we have.

First of all, after the depression of the thirties, conscription into the army absorbed a good number of young people who were leading what was considered a marginal existence at the time, but who did not necessarily have a criminal record. Gabrielle Roy's book *Bonheur d'occasion* well illustrates the fate of certain young people who were unable to fit into the dominant social milieu.[1]

Economic conditions after the war improved, and there was less unemployment and a greater sociocultural advancement for workers; the trend away from tradition, such as religious practice, however, was accompanied by a relaxation of family authority and control over minors. In short, it was as if the family in Quebec no longer considered it its duty to control the conduct and inclinations of its children. The family is no longer united to the same extent as it used to be by the need to provide for those of its young people who do not adhere to the suggested norms, and it does not consider the fact that such young people receive various social allowances as a form of disgrace. Since dropping out of school can now be compensated by the availability of continuing education, family pressure is relaxed in this domain as well. The degree of tolerance varies, of course, according to the different social classes, but the general trend seems to be undeniable.

With the relaxing of family authority, young people have turned their aggression away from parents and have directed it toward others. Thus we see the emergence of groups or gangs whose behavior embarrasses the community and thus are sought by the police.

Second, there is an increase in needs brought about by the soliciting of all potential consumers, however young, to the point where certain publicity campaigns are directed only to adolescents. Many other obvious factors can be enumerated as the immediate causes of the deviant behavior of young people, but what seems to me to be the most significant is the fact that the justice system is now taking more and more direct action with regard to the minors concerned without undertaking any studies or systematic action with respect to the families.

It is obvious that there can be no prevention among children without there being similar action vis-à-vis the parents, whose rights continue to be explicitly respected. Similarly, it is not at all certain that by applying the Juvenile Delinquents Act we can "resocialize" juvenile delinquents who are already traumatized by the injustices they have suffered and the experiences they have gone through.

Generally speaking, a juvenile delinquent is an adolescent who is late in arriving at the age of discretion and in learning how to relate to others. As such, he is rejected after a time by his peers, except those who, like him, have similar problems. He takes refuge in stubborn silence, the abuse of others, or various forms of violence. Depending on the type of relationships he adopts with others, he is called either unsociable, a manipulator, or aggressive. Basically he is dissatisfied with himself, and in spite of all attempts to improve his self-image, he feels miserable.

According to many studies, puberty, especially among boys, can be a time of particular self-dissatisfaction, a passing phase or prolonged, depending on how others treat the adolescent and how they regard his behavior during this period. In other words, the basic characteristics of juvenile delinquents exist in all children in varying degrees. Among those who lack adult care, who are badly treated or misguided, or who are poorly supervised, these characteristics become accentuated and develop into "pathologies." The biological evolution linked with puberty can be an element for release and a powerful corrective, but not necessarily so. The main distinction between children rejected by their families and in need of community care and those who come before the fourts often lies in the area of acting out, the knowledge of this act by the agents of control, such as the police or others, or the decision by the family to lodge a complaint.

Concerning comparisons that could be established between various cultural levels, the potential for individual violence among minors varies according to the general potential for violence in the population as a whole. Group violence, however, is not a function of these cultural differences, but rather is a matter of circumstances, such as passing subcultures that spread in a given community at a given time.

Unfortunately, it is easy to make generalizations regarding the phenomenon, but it is much more difficult to establish prognoses in actual cases and even more difficult to apply the appropriate treatment. An adolescent brought up in what is considered a normal way should, in principle, make progress; a child who has not had the same advantages regresses, but there is no scale by which to scientifically measure or evaluate the exact level of this regression and, even less, to offer the means to compensate for the injustices and frustrations experienced by the subject in his early childhood. In this sense, it could be claimed that juvenile delinquency, hidden or overt, is a deviation from the evolution connected with growth and not a proof of an inventive mind.

In short, the juvenile delinquent is not a whimsical being who plays tricks on adult society, but a passive or aggressive being whose behavior could be considered less a search for adventure than a flight from reality. Even though this flight is expressed in thefts, alcoholism, the use of drugs, rape or murder, the fact remains that it is a form of pathology that brings no satisfaction or gratification to the person concerned. The intervention of the system of social control can accentuate this pathology while temporarily controlling its external manifestations. Under the present conditions, an adolescent can be prevented from acting out, but this does not mean that he has changed his view of himself, his present, or his future.

Treatment and Preventive Policies

Enforcement of the legislation on the delinquency of minors makes it possible to place them "under observation," as it were, but does not necessarily mean that we educate them and help them to progress. Thus training centers receive about 5,000 to 6,000 minors annually, foster homes take in approximately 20,000, and the total number of these children placed and treated theoretically represents all the children in need of care or who have been sentenced for their behavior to live in a given place for a fixed or indeterminate length of time.

This group, however, is not representative of the true number of youngsters known to the police and the courts. Generally speaking, there are two types of statistics in this regard: police records and court records. The police take down the facts and write out the complaints. In view of their discretionary power, they can settle the matter with the parents and dismiss the case, refer it to the social services, or place the evidence before a juvenile court. The evidence is usually examined by the lawyer of the court and either rejected, returned for further investigation, or accepted and submitted to a judge. The police statistics, therefore, always show a greater number of minors apprehended than do the court records.

Regarding the latter, these are made on the basis of files, not people. Thus a juvenile delinquent, as well as a child in need of care, may have several cases pending before a court, and therefore several files. Particularly interesting in table 2-1 are the relationships that can be established between the files relating to child protection, including adoption, and those concerning juvenile delinquents.

Thus we see that on the basis of table 2-1, in all the territorial divisions in Quebec there are a greater number of files concerning juvenile delinquents than recording cases of prevention, that is, the protection of underprivileged or abandoned children. Regarding the number of juvenile delinquents heard by the Quebec juvenile courts, there were 10,637 in 1969 and 10,929 in 1973.[2] That same year, under the general heading of "socially maladjusted," we find some 26,000 minors placed in institutions and foster homes responsible to the Department of Social Affairs. Given the fact that the Quebec census for 1973 showed that there were 2,322,200 young people under the age of twenty, this means theoretically a proportion of less than 1.12 per thousand of the age group concerned.[3] In other words, about one child in a thousand requires aid and protection.

This statistic, in itself, has no significance, however, for it is only a very approximate evaluation of the application of the laws concerning children and does not show the real needs of families whose children are ill-treated, pre-delinquents, or delinquents. If we accept the fact that only one child in a thousand requires the intervention of the community, a more rigorous enforcement of the legislation should result, theoretically, in a reduction of the percentage of those considered delinquents, provided that we can succeed in establishing effective preventive policies.

In order to promote such policies and make them effective, it seems absolutely necessary to compile statistics that show actual needs as precisely

Table 2-1
Social Welfare Court Statistics, 1971

	Juvenile Delinquents Act	Youth Protection Act	Adoption	Provincial Statutes	Bylaws	Total
1. Gaspe-Bonaventure	263	69	72	59	–	463
2. Rimouski-Kamouraska	557	87	142	–	–	786
3. Chicoutimi-Roberval-Chibougamau	1,001	301	151	–	–	1,453
4. Trois-Rivières-St-Maurice	1,959	126	240	–	–	2,325
5. Drummond-Richelieu-St-Hyacinthe	453	373	114	98	17	1,055
6. Beauce-Megantic-Arthabaska	404	199	15	79	–	697
7. St-François-Bedford	842	455	176	–	–	1,473
8. Iberville-Beauharnois	1,049	275	96	–	–	1,420
9. Terrebonne	1,828	529	80	–	–	2,437
10. Joliette	459	355	73	–	–	887
11. Hull-Pontiac-Labelle	1,257	382	194	222	84	2,139
12. Abitibi-Temiscamingue-Rouyn-Noranda	1,281	139	104	–	–	1,524
13. Saguenay-Hauterive-Mingan	710	46	73	36	3	868
14. Montreal (Verdun-Pointe-Claire)	8,566	1,975	2,124	694	649	14,008
15. Quebec-Montmagny	1,506	566	562	–	–	2,634
Totals	22,135	5,877	4,216	1,188	753	34,169
Statistics for the year 1970	19,176	5,837	3,735	1,201	667	30,616
Increase or decrease over 1970	2,959 (A)	40 (A)	481 (A)	13 (D)	86 (A)	3,553 (A)

as possible. In this regard, there are two possible approaches. The first is to make evaluations and projections on the basis of a time perspective. By studying the data for the last 10 years, for example, the lows and highs can be isolated and the averages taken. Applying the totals thus obtained to the demographic evolution makes it possible theoretically to foresee how acute the problem will be during the coming years and to plan for the organization of the necessary services.

Because of a number of variables, however, such planning is necessarily somewhat risky. It is almost impossible to predict whether there will be an acceleration or gradual lessening of family instability, with its consequent recourse to the state services concerning the care of the children. For example, there could be increased resistance to the socioeconomic pressures of the single-parent family, or on the other hand, the latter could more and more frequently refuse responsibility for the youngsters. Similarly, it is possible that the single-parent family will disappear in Quebec, or again, it might become more commonplace. There are sufficient arguments to uphold one or the other of these two hypotheses.

For all these reasons, I believe that evaluations of the yearly statistics for set periods of time are not as basic as those of an analysis of the phenomenon at a given moment according to territorial districts and neighborhoods of large cities. A statistical model of this kind is perfectly feasible, although it has not been systematically adopted to date, possibly because there are no parallel statistics compiled by the federal government, which makes a distinction only between the provinces. We might add that Canadian statistics do not take into account the cases of children in need of protection because there is no uniform legislation throughout Canada in this area; this a survey is made only of juvenile delinquency.

The regional and neighborhood approach, therefore, applies more to a model adopted to the needs of children in Quebec. The compilation of such a model is possible on the basis of both police and judicial statistics. The police services record all cases concerning minors, according to the hour, day, month, and radius of action of each police station, all registered within clearly marked boundaries.

Thus through my research, it is possible to establish the hours and days of the week in which a specific concentration of infractions are committed and their perpetrators apprehended by the police.[4] The numbers 1, 2, or 3 indicate the results that are obtained on the basis of the daily records of the Montreal Police for 1969, 1970, and 1971. The constants they reflect are sufficiently interesting, I feel, for us to try to systematically adopt a similar plan of analysis for the general data.

Similarly, a study of the statistics of the juvenile courts, according to territorial district and including the data concerning children being protected under the provincial laws and juvenile delinquents, would make it possible to pinpoint the areas where there are the greatest number of youth problems.

In principle, juvenile delinquency is more concentrated in the urbanized areas, but this does not prove that, considering the total population of the same age groups, it is not greater elsewhere. According to the findings of my research, for example, the distribution would be that shown in table 2-2.

The studies done by Marc LeBlanc, one of the rare Quebec criminologists whose specific interest is statistical analyses of juvenile delinquency, confirms my hypotheses and results. In his report "La délinquance juvénile an Québec," published by the Department of Social Affairs in 1977, Marc LeBlanc writes:

> It is clearly shown that the most populous regions are also the most delinquent, . . . but socio-economic regions differ in delinquency and population [free translation].

He mainly analyzes the indicators relating to juvenile delinquency, and considering the powers of judges to hear the case of a minor under the provincial Youth Protection Act rather than the Juvenile Delinquents Act, no matter what the act committed, it is practically impossible, in my opinion, to determine the actual situation regarding the maladjustment of minors. The deterioration of a child's personality, a determining factor in the elaboration of prevention policies, may be more marked in the case of the child defined in the statistics as having need of protection than in that of the adolescent known to the police and the court as a juvenile delinquent.

Failures Reported

Concerning juvenile delinquents, enforcement of the law is largely a matter of the means and services available. This explains the fact that the measures ordered by judges are often contradictory, as can be seen by the following fourteen dossiers from the files of minors, dating from 1974.

The young people concerned were all finally referred to an adult court after having been treated under the sociolegal system for several years, sometimes as children in need of protection, sometimes as juvenile delinquents. In terms of percentages, this is a very small group, but the dossiers illustrate particularly well the failure of the application of the legislation on young people. Since these are adolescents who were referred by juvenile judges to the Court of Sessions, the measures taken are specified, which is not always the case for those who continue to appear before the Juvenile Court. True, adult offenders often admit that for several years they were "treated" as children in need of protection or as juvenile delinquents, but their files are not available, since, according to law, once the prophetic age of majority has been reached, no record can be kept of the judgments passed when a person was still a minor.

In other words, the only way to fully illustrate the failures of the application of the laws concerning minors, based on official records, is by analyzing the cases of adolescents referred to a different court. The significance of these, despite the small percentage, is extremely important for an understanding of what children go through when their families cannot, or do not, fulfill their role.

Table 2-2
Proportion of Children Judged, By Territorial District, Quebec, 1979

Territorial District	Total Population (0 to 17 Years)	Children Protected and Adopted (No. of Files)	Delinquents (No. of Files)
Iberville-Beauharnois	52,559	371	1,049
Terrebonne	94,670	609	1,828
Trois-Rivieres-St-Maurice	121,883	366	1,959
Saguenay-Hauterive-Mingan	55,355	119	749
Drummond-Richelieu-St-Hyacinthe	68,522	487	568
Joliette	65,191	428	459
Chicoutimi-Roberval-Chibougamau	118,754	452	1,001
St-François-Bedford	127,780	631	842
Hull-Pontiac-Labelle	192,286	576	1,583
Gaspé-Bonaventure	44,818	141	322
Montreal	363,204	4,099	9,909
Abitibi-Temiscamingue-Rouyn-Noranda	153,211	243	1,281
Quebec-Montmagny	278,110	1,128	1,506
Beauce-Megantic-Arthabaska	73,923	214	483
Rimouski-Kamouraska	98,768	229	557

Note: Data classified in decreasing order.

Offenses

Offenses

a.

b.

M   T   W   T   F   S   S

M   T   W   T   F   S   S

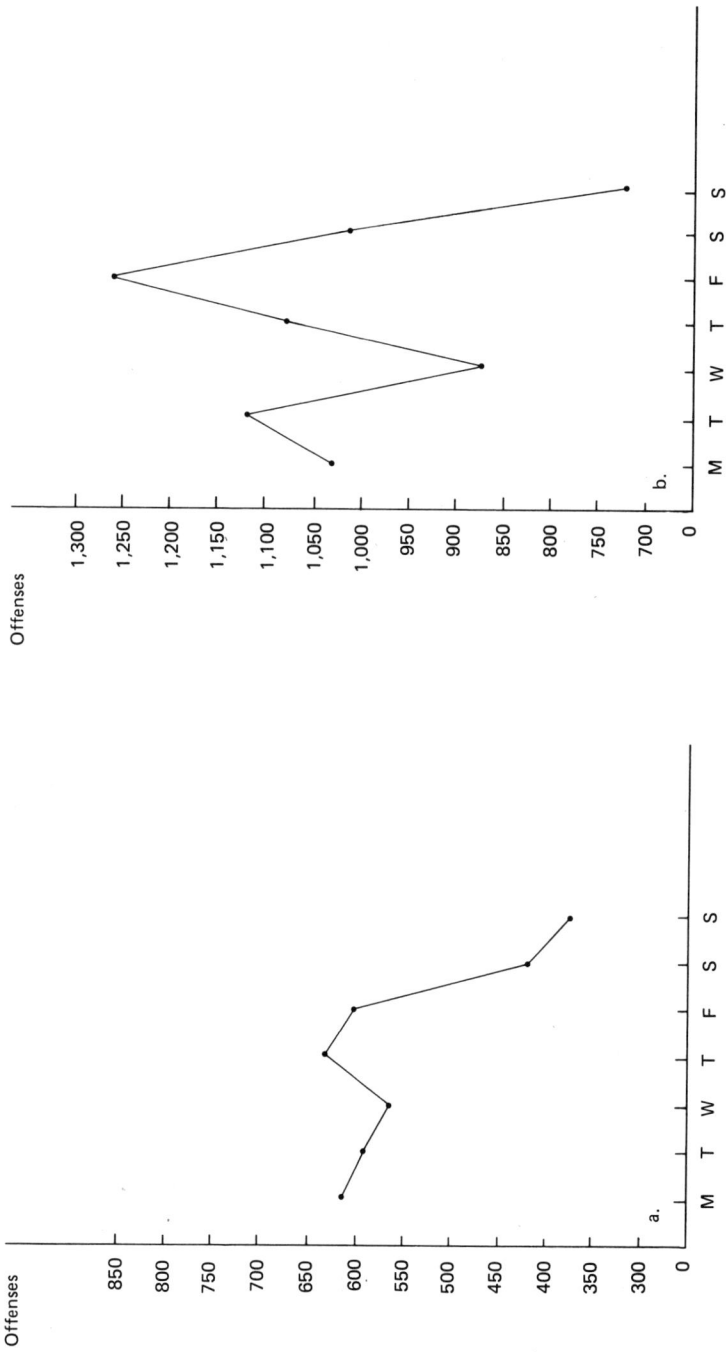

Source: Montreal Police, 1969, 1970.

Figure 2-1. Juvenile Delinquency According to Days of the Week: (a) 1969, (b) 1970

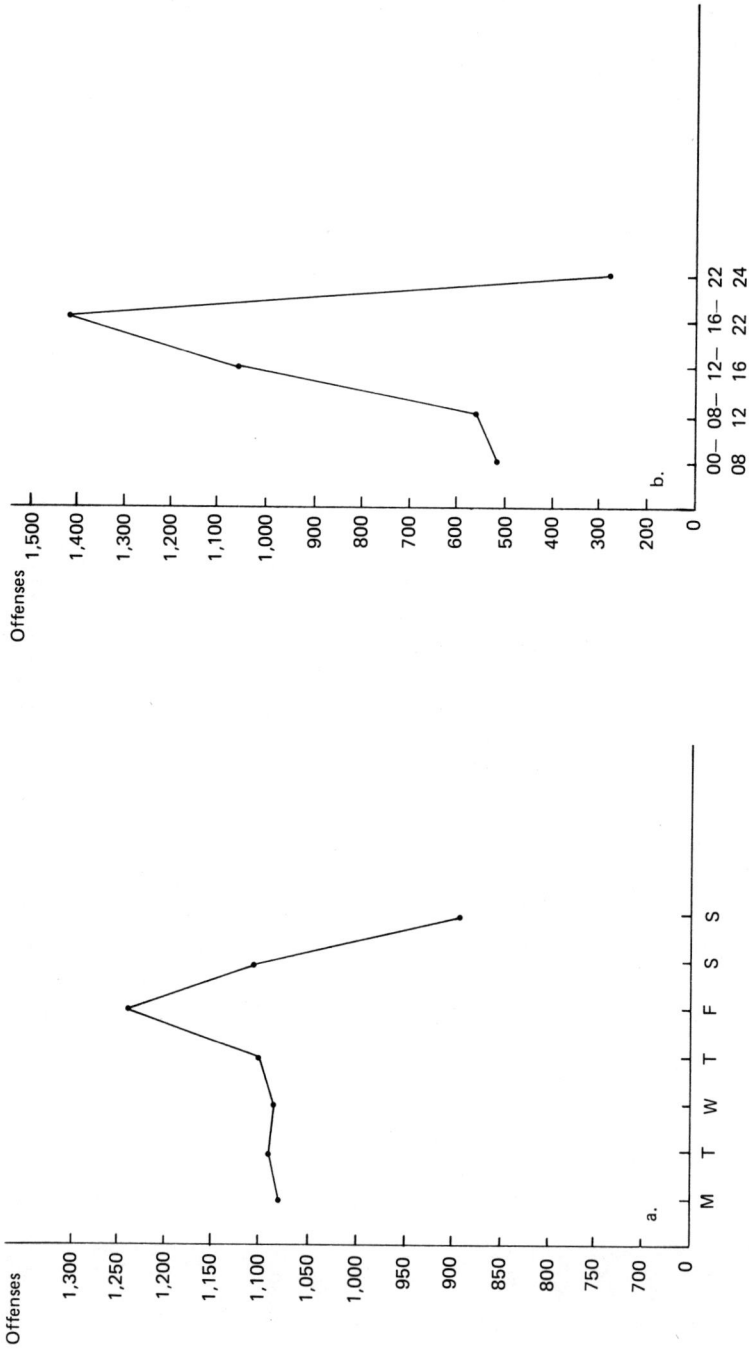

Offenses

Offenses

a.

M   T   W   T   F   S   S

b.

00— 08— 12— 16— 22
08   12   16   22   24

Source: Montreal Police, 1969 and 1971.

Figure 2-2. Juvenile Delinquency (a) According to Days of the Week, (b) According to Hour

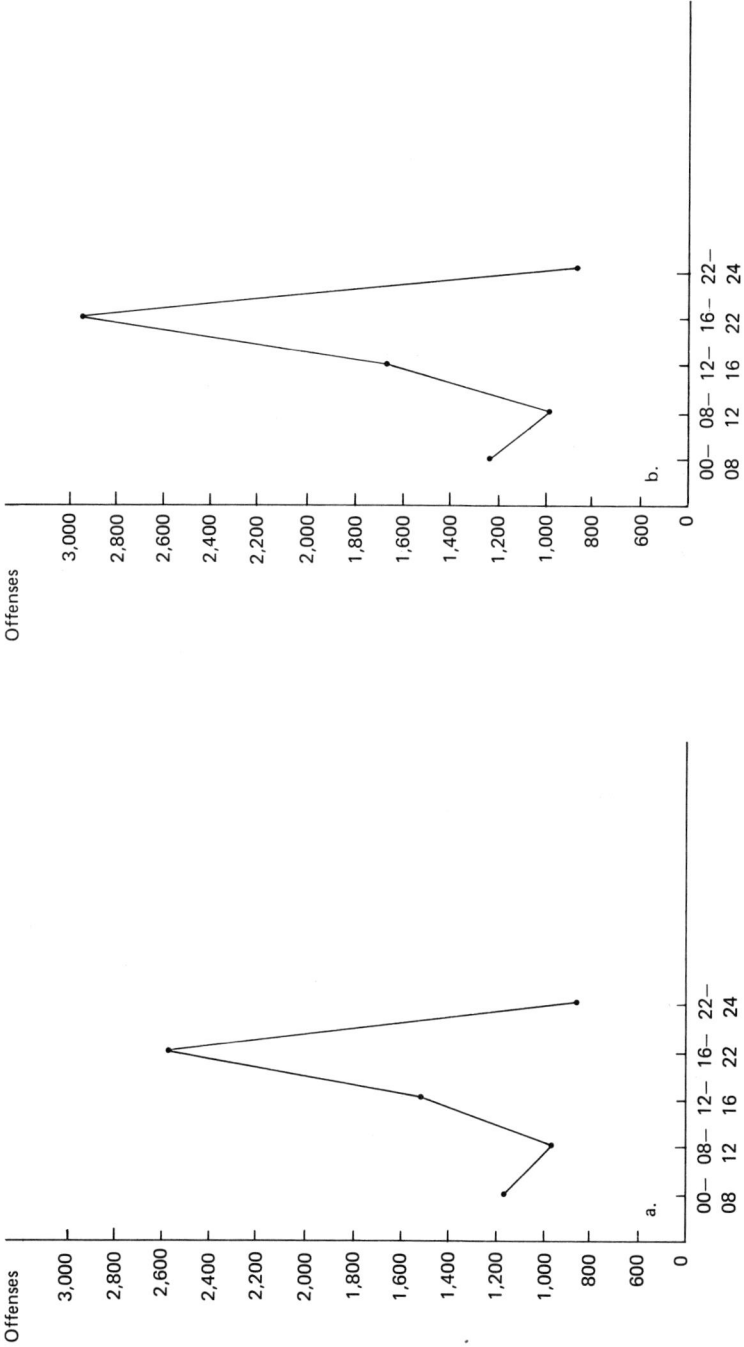

Figure 2-3. Juvenile Delinquency According to Hour: (a) 1970, (b) 1971

Source: Montreal Police, 1970 and 1971.

Dossier No. 1

Date of Birth: 1959

Sex: Male

Infractions Ascribed by the Social Welfare Court to the Delinquent prior to the Referral	Dates of Appearances	Decisions Made by the Social Welfare Court prior to the Referral	Infractions for which He Was Referred to Adult Court
Theft and receipt of stolen goods	14/06/67 (8 years)	During the holidays, he will go to Camp Pie X in St. Donat from 23/06/67 to 04/09/67	
Theft and receipt of a bicycle	29/06/67	Dismissed from camp indefinitely; 28/08/67, at home; placed in the Montreal Catholic Orphanage 05/09/67; 4 escapes; not accepted for the school year 1968–1969; 29/06/68, escapes again, returned home; 15/07/68 to 13/09/68, Auberge des Copains at St. Donat; 01/10/68, at home; goes to school; 04/11/68, no longer attends school; Mtl. Catholic School Board sends the child to his parents; referred to Dominique Savio; 29/04/69, returned to his parents.	
Burglary and receipt ($280)	02/05/69	Already on probation; postponed indefinitely; St. Vallier; 29/05/69, returned to the family while waiting admission to Camp Sacré-Coeur du Centre Mgr Forget; did not go back to camp in August.	
Theft and receipt of a bicycle	18/10/69	Appearance postponed: did not obey the order to appear.	
Theft and receipt of bicycle ($45)	11/06/70	13/07/70, spent the summer at Camp Sacré-Coeur; September: Centre Mgr Forget	
Loafing in public places	14/01/71	Postponed indefinitely; placed in charge of his mother; May 1971 the PO will take steps to have the MCSB accept the child; on probation.	
Municipal bylaw (disturbing the peace)	14/05/71	Warrant to appear before the court; 17/05/71 the child appears; on probation; PO has great difficulty finding institutions in view of past failures.	

Disturbing the peace (M.B.)	21/02/72	Postponed indefinitely; probation; 06/02/72, leaves home (is 13 years old); 08/02/72, warrant; 11/02/72, returns on his own.
Petty theft ($10)	29/03/72	Does not attend school; because of lack of discipline, the school refuses to take him back; postponed sine die; probation.
Loitering at night	09/05/72	Issued a summons; 29/05/72, appears under another complaint; sine die; probation.
Loitering at night	14/05/72	Idem
Robbery and receipt ($3.25)	29/05/72	Sine die; continued probation; probation during the summer of 1972.
Attempted auto theft	15/08/72	Summons to the child and parents to appear; 21/08/72, order to appear; 28/08/72, detention; 05/09/72, trial: child given the benefit of the doubt; complaint dismissed; 29/11/72, returned to his parents on condition that he behave and return to school; 04/12/72, ran away from home: order to appear.
Immoral conduct	06/02/73	Appeared before the court: postponed sine die; probation continued; declared juvenile delinquent; does not go to school; Preventive detention until 19/03/73; 19/03/73, returned to the mother by the court: rules of conduct laid down for the child.
Robbery and receipt of stolen goods ($400)	06/04/73	Preventive detention until 18/04/73; 18/04/73, reevaluation clinic; preventive detention until 18/05/73; 18/05/73, probation; 17/07/73, complaint dismissed: lack of proof.
Compound robbery	01/06/73	Summons; 05/06/73, parents moved; order for the child to appear; 19/06/73, preventive detention: postponed sine die; 05/07/73, detention while awaiting placement; toward mid-June, escaped from St. Vallier; order for the child to appear.

Dossier No. 1 continued

Infractions Ascribed by the Social Welfare Court to the Delinquent prior to the Referral	Dates of Appearances	Decisions Made by the Social Welfare Court prior to the Referral	Infractions for which He Was Referred to Adult Court
Theft and receipt of truck	11/02/74	Concealment only; detention while waiting detention at Boscoville: postponed sine die; 14/02/74, escapes; order to appear; 22/02/74, detention; 26/02/75, escapes; order to appear.	
Burglary (less than $200)	15/03/74	Detention; appearance postponed in view of provisions in another dossier.	
Burglary ($375)	15/03/74	Detention: Berthelet until 13/05/74.	
Attempted auto theft	29/03/74	Trial postponed; 28/04/74, escapes; order to appear; 31/05/74, detention at St. Hyacinthe until 27/06/74 (child 15 years old); 27/06/74, request for transfer refused; last chance: returned to Boscoville.	
Theft and receipt of motorcycle	21/05/74	27/06/74, postponed sine die; 14/07/74, dossier reopened; 12/02/75, referred to Court of Sessions.	Case referred 12/02/75
Burglary and receipt ($25)	21/05/74	Idem	Case referred 12/02/75
Theft and receipt of motorcycle	21/05/74	Idem	Case referred 12/02/75
Theft and receipt of motorcycle	21/05/74	Idem	Case referred 12/02/75
Theft and receipt of motorcycle	21/05/74	Idem	Case referred 12/02/75
Theft and receipt of motorbike	21/05/74	Idem; 21/06/74, sent to Boscoville; 02/07/74, escapes; order to appear; 04/07/74, Berthelet until 08/07/74 for examination; child refuses to return to Boscoville; wants to be submitted to court; judge annuls placement at Boscoville; reopens previous dossiers requesting change of sentence; 08/07/74, the court accepts the motion to change; asks admission to l'Institut Pinel; 08/07/74, escapes from the court.	Case referred 12/02/75
Theft and receipt of motorbike	06/08/74	Committed to Parthenais for transfer to St. Hyacinthe; 18/09/74, detention at St. Hyacinthe due to no response from Pinel; 29/11/74, examination at Pinel;	

Theft and receipt of auto	27/12/74	returned to St. Hyacinthe; 03/12/74, on recommendation of the Pinel psychiatrist, placed on probation in his mother's charge.	Case referred 12/02/75
		24/12/74, detention; 28/12/74, escapes from St. Vallier; summons; 17/01/75, released on probation because working; appearance postponed sine die 17/01/75	
Disturbing the peace (M.B.)	17/01/75	Idem; since referred in other dossiers, appearance postponed sine die.	
Theft and receipt of auto	11/03/75	See above	Case referred 12/02/75
Theft and receipt of auto	17/06/75	Referred	Case referred 17/06/75

Child's Attitude in Protective Environment

Report from Foster Homes	*Report from Training Schools*
None	None

Preventive Detention

05/09/72 to 29/11/72 (age 13)
06/02/73 to 19/03/73 (age 14)
06/04/73 to 18/04/73 (age 14)
18/04/73 to 18/05/73 (age 14)
19/06/73 to ?/06/73 (age 14)
18/09/73 to 18/12/73 (age 14)

Child's School Situation

Frequent changes of school; absenteeism; behind in schooling; at about third grade level.

Child's Family Situation

Father an epileptic; mother works part time; eight children at home.

Reasons for Referral to the Court of Sessions of the Peace

Thirteen periods of detention
Twenty-nine complaints laid
Sixteen escapes
Six institutions refused to accept the child.
All efforts at rehabilitation failed.
Use of the entire resources of the court.
The interest of the child and society: offences not very serious, but numerous.

Dossier No. 2

Date of Birth: July 27, 1959

Sex: Male

Infractions Imputed by the Social Welfare Court to the Delinquent prior to the Referral	Dates of Appearances	Decisions Made by the Social Welfare Court prior to the Referral	Infractions for which He Was Referred to Adult Court
Disturbing the peace	06/03/73 (age 14)	Postponed sine die in view of request for protection; demand for protection under art. 15 by the mother (child unable to be controlled, signs of predelinquency, plays truant, sniffs glue, commits petty theft); detention while awaiting probation; clinical examination; 03/04/73, desertion from Berthelet (age 14); 11/04/73, returns home conditionally (attends school, sees a doctor about his use of glue); 15/05/73, good report from probation officer; 03/12/73, postponed sine die.	
Attempted theft	19/09/73	Detention; 20/09/73, escapes; summons issued; 26/09/73, detention at Berthelet; 01/10/73, escapes; summons issued; 10/10/73, detention; 03/12/73, postponed sine die.	
Theft and receipt ($200)	02/10/73	Warrant because he did not appear; 10/10/73, detention; escape from Berthelet 18/10/73; summons; 29/11/73, kept in detention at the request of the PO; 03/12/73, appeared before court: returned home conditionally; 04/02/73, runs away from home; seriously addicted to drugs; summons; 19/02/74, placement considered; detention because exposed to physical danger (Berthelet); 10/04/74, temporary discharge from 11 to 16/04/74; 18/04/74, child did not return to Berthelet; summons.	

Offense	Date	Description
Shoplifting ($29.95)	14/06/74	Detention, 17/07/74, postponed sine die; request admission to Mont St. Antoine; 29/07/74, released on parole; 02/08/74, ran away from home; summons; 05/09/74, brought to court; detention while awaiting MSA; 18/09/74, admitted to MSA; several escapes from MSA; 30/09/74, 21/10/74, 01/11/74, 04/11/74, 14/11/74; no longer motivated to return there; detention; 20/12/74, released on parole.
Conspiring to commit compound robbery	28/02/75	25/02/75, summons because he did not appear and did not obey the conditions; 28/02/75, investigation for referral; preventive detention; 25/04/75, complaint dismissed because he pleaded guilty to compound robbery.
Idem	Idem	Idem
Idem	Idem	Idem
Idem	Idem	Idem
Idem	Idem	Idem
Idem	Idem	Idem
Idem	Idem	Idem
Idem	Idem	Idem
Idem	Idem	Idem
Compound robbery and conspiracy		Detention until 06/03/75; inquiry on referral; 03/03/75, escapes from St. Vallier; summons; 26/03/75, St. Hyacinthe.
Compound robbery ($521), revolver		Idem; postponed sine die 25/04/75 because the child is at MSA.
Compound robbery ($137), revolver		Idem

Dossier No. 2 continued

Infractions Imputed by the Social Welfare Court to the Delinquent prior to the Referral	Dates of Appearances	Decisions Made by the Social Welfare Court prior to the Referral	Infractions for which He Was Referred to Adult Court
Compound robbery ($233), .22 revolver		Idem; the dossier will be reopened 10/10/75 for referral.	Case referred 21/10/75
Compound robbery ($550), chromium-plated revolver		Idem, the dossier will be reopened 10/10/75.	Case referred 21/10/75
Compound robbery ($35)		Idem	Case referred 21/10/75
Compound robbery ($64), revolver	28/02/75	See above.	Case referred 21/10/75
Compound robbery ($165)	Idem	Idem	Case referred 21/10/75
Compound robbery ($275)	Idem	Idem	Case referred 21/10/75
Compound robbery ($67), .22 revolver	Idem	Idem	Case referred 21/10/75
Compound robbery, revolver	Idem	Idem	Case referred 21/10/75
Compound robbery ($435)	Idem	Idem	Case referred 21/10/75
Compound robbery ($300)	Idem	Idem	Case referred 21/10/75
Compound robbery ($109)	Idem	Idem	Case referred 21/10/75
Compound robbery ($600), .22 revolver	Idem	Idem	Case referred 21/10/75
Compound robbery	Idem	Idem	Case referred 21/10/75

Offense	Date	Disposition	Referral
Compound robbery ($800), revolver	26/03/75	Detention at St. Hyacinthe; inquiry on referral postponed until 02/04/75, St. Vallier; 15/05/75, motion for referral presented; 15/04/75, rejected because all resources have not been exhausted; detention until 17/04/75; 25/04/75, postponed sine die because motivated to return to MSA.	Case referred 21/10/75
Compound robbery ($200), .16 caliber sawed-off shotgun	26/03/75	See above.	Case referred 21/10/75
Conspiracy to commit compound robbery	Idem	Complaint dismissed because he pleaded guilty to compound robbery 25/04/75.	
Conspiracy to commit compound robbery	Idem	Idem	
Compound robbery ($125), rifle	02/04/75	Detention St. Hyacinthe 24/04/75; decision postponed sine die.	Case referred 21/10/75
Compound robbery ($550)	Idem	Idem; clinical report: high anxiety level, average I.Q., no father figure, manipulator, acting out an attempt to escape his anxiety.	Case referred 21/10/75
Compound robbery ($800)	Idem	Idem	Case referred 21/10/75
Compound robbery ($185)	Idem	Idem	Case referred 21/10/75
Compound robbery ($480)	Idem	Postponed sine die: to MSA.	Case referred 21/10/75
Attempted compound robbery	Idem	25/04/75, decision postponed sine die.	Case referred 21/10/75
Compound robbery ($175)	Idem	Idem	Case referred 21/10/75
Compound robbery ($300), chromium-plated revolver	Idem	Idem	Case referred 21/10/75
Compound robbery ($342), imitation weapon	10/10/75	Idem	Case referred 21/10/75

Dossier No. 2 continued

Infractions Imputed by the Social Welfare Court to the Delinquent prior to the Referral	Dates of Appearances	Decisions Made by the Social Welfare Court prior to the Referral	Infractions for which He Was Referred to Adult Court
Compound robbery ($300)	Idem	Idem	Case referred 21/10/75
Compound robbery ($250), imitation weapon	Idem	Idem	Case referred 21/10/75
Compound robbery ($40)	Idem	Idem	Case referred 21/10/75
Compound robbery ($600), imitation weapon	Idem	Idem	Case referred 21/10/75
Compound robbery ($100)	Idem	Idem	Case referred 21/10/75
Compound robbery ($40)	Idem	Idem	Case referred 21/10/75
Compound robbery ($167)	Idem	Idem	Case referred 21/10/75
Compound robbery ($450)	Idem	Idem	Case referred 21/10/75
Compound robbery ($200), revolver	Idem	Idem	Case referred 21/10/75
Compound robbery ($400), revolver	Idem	Idem	Case referred 21/10/75
Compound robbery ($310)	Idem	Idem	Case referred 21/10/75
Compound robbery ($70), revolver	Idem	Idem	Case referred 21/10/75

Compound robbery ($50), chromium-plated revolver	24/04/75	Idem	Case referred 21/10/75
Compound robbery ($212), chromium-plated revolver	Idem	Idem	Case referred 21/10/75
Compound robbery ($114), chromium-plated revolver	24/04/75	Idem; desertion from MSA, 25/04/75; summons; 28/04/75, St. Hyacinthe; 01/05/75, placement at MSA annulled; clinical report: neurotic conflicts of a hysterical nature; detention at Berthelet while awaiting admission to Boscoville; 14/06/75, escapes; summons; 15/07/75, new complaint; Parthenais because of numerous previous escapes.	Case referred 21/10/75
Disturbing the peace (M.B.)	15/07/75	Detention at Parthenais; 17/07/75, appearance postponed sine die; 12/08/75, Boscoville (age 16) for an indefinite period; 13/08/75, escapes; 20/08/75, runs away again; summons.	
Breaking and entering with intent	10/10/75	Detention; referred 21/10/75 to maximum security.	Case referred 21/10/75
Theft and receipt ($50)	10/10/75	Idem	Case referred 21/10/75
Compound robbery ($550), imitation weapon	10/10/75	Idem	Case referred 21/10/75
Compound robbery ($311), revolver	10/10/75	Idem	Case referred 21/10/75
Compound robbery ($20)	10/10/75	Idem	Case referred 21/10/75
Compound robbery ($286)	Idem	Idem	Case referred 21/10/75
Compound robbery ($187)	Idem	Idem	Case referred 21/10/75
Compound robbery ($265), revolver	Idem	Idem	Case referred 21/10/75

Dossier No. 2 continued

Child's Attitude in Protective Environment

Report from Foster Homes	*Report from Training Schools*
None	None

Preventive Detention

06/03/73 to 11/04/73 (age 13)
29/11/73 to 02/12/73 (age 14)
19/02/74 to 10/04/74 (age 14)
05/09/74 to 18/09/74 (age 15)
15/04/75 to 25/04/75 (age 15)

Child's School Situation

Frequent changes of school; absenteeism; behind in schooling; repeated fourth and fifth grades.

Child's Family Situation

Father deceased; natural child; one sister at home; raised by his grandparents until the age of 10; at the age of 7 was placed in an orphanage for 3 years.

Reasons for Referral to the Court of Sessions of the Peace

No progress was made as a result of the measures taken. No other valid measure was available to the Court.

The good of the child.

Dossier No. 3

Date of Birth: May 21, 1959

Sex: Male

Infractions Ascribed by the Social Welfare Court to the Delinquent prior to the Referral	Dates of Appearances	Decisions Made by the Social Welfare Court prior to the Referral	Infractions for which He Was Referred to Adult Court
Burglary and receipt ($35)	21/07/67 (age 8)	06/11/64, request for protection, under article 15; 24/11/64, postponed sine die.	
		Not declared a juvenile delinquent because of age (8 years); placed in his mother's care; postponed sine die.	
Burglary and receipt ($30)	21/07/67	Idem	
Breaking and entering with intent	30/08/67	Appearance postponed until 12/09/67; 26/09/67, adjourned sine die.	
Breaking and entering with intent	Idem	Idem	
Burglary and receipt ($3.00)	Idem	Idem	
Burglary and receipt ($17)	Idem	Idem	
Burglary and receipt ($15)	Idem	Idem	
Breaking and entering	18/10/67	Already in the hands of social workers; adjourned sine die.	
Burglary and receipt ($20)	Idem	Idem	

Dossier No. 3 continued

Infractions Ascribed by the Social Welfare Court to the Delinquent prior to the Referral	Dates of Appearances	Decisions Made by the Social Welfare Court prior to the Referral	Infractions for which He Was Referred to Adult Court
Theft and receipt (bicycle)	31/05/68	Adjourned sine die.	
Burglary and receipt ($151)	31/05/68	Adjourned sine die.	
Burglary and receipt ($157)	31/05/68	Clinical examination ordered at the Clinique de l'enfant et de la famille; adjourned sine die (age 9).	
Theft and receipt ($35)	28/06/68	A social worker takes him to school every morning; he was taken to visit the detention cells; adjourned sine die.	
Breaking and entering with intent	10/07/68	Placed at Notre Dame du Perpétuel Secours from 10 to 22/07/68.	
Burglary and receipt ($120)	13/08/69	In detention until August 25; postponed sine die; 04/09/69, placed at Notre Dame du Bel-Amour; on probation.	
Burglary and receipt ($215)	09/07/70	Adjourned sine die; returned to Notre Dame du Bel-Amour for summer camp; released conditionally.	
Burglary and receipt ($70)	09/07/70	Idem	
Burglary and receipt	09/07/70	See above; adjourned sine die.	
Burglary and receipt ($25)	26/07/71	Idem	

Burglary receipt ($455)	26/07/71	Idem
Burglary and receipt ($108)	26/07/71	Idem
Burglary and receipt ($206)	26/07/71	Idem
Burglary and receipt ($4.19)	07/09/71	Detention until 08/09/71; adjourned sine die; put in charge of the probation service for placement; foster home no. 1.
Breaking and entering with intent	07/09/71	Idem; 30/09/71, good report from foster home; runs away from foster home 21/07/72; warrant issued.
Burglary and receipt ($75)	17/08/72	25/08/72, under detention once more; postponed sine die; Detention until 12/10/72; returned to his mother; intensive supervision on probation.
		From 17/10/72 to ?/01/73, goes to school regularly but stays away frequently; 11/01/73, leaves school; summons; in detention until admitted to Notre Dame de la Merci (Huberdeau) in February 1973.
Breaking and entering with intent	25/04/73	Adjourned sine die.
Breaking and entering with intent	03/07/73	Adjourned sine die.
Breaking and entering with intent	03/07/73	Idem
Idem	Idem	Idem
Idem	Idem	Idem
Burglary and receipt ($24)	13/08/73	Idem
Breaking and entering with intent	13/08/73	Idem; the child had run away from D'Huberdean four times (four summons were issued).

Dossier No. 3 continued

Infractions Ascribed by the Social Welfare Court to the Delinquent prior to the Referral	Dates of Appearances	Decisions Made by the Social Welfare Court prior to the Referral	Infractions for which He Was Referred to Adult Court
		17/05/74, released from Notre Dame de la Merci; 31/05/74, committed to Mont St. Antoine (the child is 14); runs away 10/07/74; summons 20/07/74.	
Burglary and receipt ($700)	04/09/74	In detention; adjourned sine die.	
Burglary and receipt ($500)	04/09/74	Idem	
Burglary and receipt ($65)	Idem	Idem	
Burglary and receipt ($75)	Idem	Idem	
Burglary and receipt ($360)	Idem	Idem	
Burglary and receipt ($250)	Idem	Idem	
Burglary and receipt ($1,900)	Idem	Idem	
		24/10/74, does not want to return to Mont St. Antoine; placed on parole; 16/01/75, very good report from the PO; 17/04/75, lost his job.	
Burglary and receipt ($1,165)	23/06/75	In detention; is to be placed on parole 04/07/75.	Case referred 30/10/75
Burglary and receipt ($100)	23/06/75	Idem	Case referred 30/10/75
Burglary and receipt	23/06/75	Idem	Case referred 30/10/75

Burglary and receipt ($671)	23/06/75	See above.	Case referred 30/10/75
Driving without a permit	23/06/75	Postponed sine die.	Case referred 30/10/75
Breaking and entering with intent	23/06/75	Detention; 04/07/75 released on parole.	Case referred 30/10/75
Burglary and receipt ($25)	23/06/75	Idem	Case referred 30/10/75
Burglary and receipt ($240)	Idem	Idem	Case referred 30/10/75
Burglary and receipt ($650)	Idem	Idem	Case referred 30/10/75
Burglary and receipt ($2,185)	Idem	Idem	Case referred 30/10/75
Burglary and receipt ($3,829)	Idem	Idem	Case referred 30/10/75
Burglary and receipt ($745)	Idem	Idem	Case referred 30/10/75
Burglary and receipt ($102)	Idem	Idem	Case referred 30/10/75
Burglary and receipt ($102)	Idem	Idem	Case referred 30/10/75
Burglary and receipt ($40)	Idem	Idem	Case referred 30/10/75
Burglary and receipt ($39)	Idem	Idem	Case referred 30/10/75

Dossier No. 3 continued

Infractions Ascribed by the Social Welfare Court to the Delinquent prior to the Referral	Dates of Appearances	Decisions Made by the Social Welfare Court prior to the Referral	Infractions for which He Was Referred to Adult Court
Attempt at breaking and entering with intent	23/06/75	Idem	Case referred 30/10/75
Burglary and receipt ($20)	Idem	Idem	Case referred 30/10/75
Burglary and receipt ($200)	Idem	Idem	Case referred 30/10/75
Burglary and receipt ($300)	Idem	Idem	Case referred 30/10/75
Burglary and receipt ($8.00)	Idem	Idem	Case referred 30/10/75
Burglary and receipt ($1,368)	03/09/75	Idem	Case referred 30/10/75
Burglary and receipt ($65,900)	03/09/75	Detention until 04/09/ ? at the Parthenais Center (because he ran away from St. Vallier 21/08/75 and there was no room at Berthelet); 04/09/75 Cowansville Prison	

Child's Attitude in Protective Environment

Report from Foster Homes	Report from Training Schools
30/09/71, getting along well; registered at school.	04/09/69, Notre Dame du Bel Amour; boards week-days
21/07/72, ran away from foster home.	03/03/70, sent home because he was not up to second grade standard; readmitted in July 1970 to summer

Preventive Detention

25/08/72 to 12/10/72 (age 12)
11/01/73 to February/73 (age 12)

camp and for the school year; ran away in August and in September 1970; after September 1970, during the week he started to bring back small objects: radios, watches; when questioned, his parents defended him.

Notre Dame de la Merci (Huberdeau); 4 escapes: February 1973, June 1973, October 1973, Beginning of 1974.

Child's Family Situation

Father a criminal (the last infraction referred: burglary and possession of $65,900.); was committed in the company of the father.

Parents are alcoholics; three sisters; four brothers.

Child's School Situation

Repeated first and second year

Reason for Referral to the Court of Sessions of the Peace

Infractions numerous and always more and more serious.
Had been through all the institutions.
Clinical report: has no sense of guilt; confirmed delinquent; can no longer be treated in an institution under the jurisdiction of the Social Welfare Court.

Dossier No. 4

Date of Birth: September 26, 1958

Sex: Male

Infractions Ascribed by the Social Welfare Court to the Delinquent prior to the Referral	Dates of Appearances	Decisions Made by the Social Welfare Court prior to the Referral	Infractions for which He Was Referred to Adult Court
	27/03/72 (age 14)	Request made for protection under article 15; the child had run away from home because he had been beaten, exposed to physical danger; 07/04/72, in detention; 12/04/72, released; 01/05/72 and 11/09/72, good reports from the mother: goes to school; postponed sine die.	
Interfering with the duties of the police	05/01/73	Seen by specialists at Douglas Hospital; follow-up by social worker; goes to school; adjourned sine die.	
Theft and possession of motorcycle	13/07/73	Already on probation; adjourned sine die.	
Burglary and receipt	?/08/73	Sine die.	
Burglary and receipt	10/10/73	Detention until 18/10/73; adjourned sine die (will be referred on this dossier, 23/05/75; 18/10/75, released and taken to the Boys' Farm and Training School.	Case referred 23/05/75
Theft and receipt ($63.70)	05/04/74	In detention; adjourned sine die.	
Theft and receipt ($5.00)	05/04/74	Idem	
Theft and receipt ($30)	05/04/74	Idem; 28/04/74, runs away from Boys' Farm.	
Attempted fraud (credit card)	01/05/74	Postponed sine die.	

Offense	Date	Disposition	
Burglary and receipt ($200)	24/08/74	21/05/74, returns to BF; spends weekends at home; 04/06/74, runs away from BF; returns 12/06/74; 11/07/74 runs away; in detention until 02/08/74; escapes from St. Vallier; detention until 06/09/74.	
Theft and receipt ($150)	26/11/74	Postponed sine die; 12/09/74, returns to BF (in closed unit); 14/09/74, runs away; 07/10/74, returns to BF.	
Burglary and receipt ($3,868)	28/01/75	Detention until 04/12/74, sine die because in institution; 07/12/74, escapes from St. Vallier; 09/12/74, returns to BF.	
Burglary and receipt ($163)	28/01/75	Postponed sine die.	
Burglary and receipt ($38)	28/01/75	Postponed sine die.	
Burglary and receipt ($150)	17/03/75	02/02/75, escapes from BF; returns 25/02/75 (the child is 17); Escapes March 10.	
Burglary and receipt ($325)	18/03/75	18/03/75, escapes from St. Vallier; summons issued; appearance; 25/03/75, escapes from St. Vallier; summons issued; 01/04/75, detention (arrested on other charge).	Case referred 23/05/75
Burglary and receipt ($175)	18/03/75	Idem	Case referred 23/05/75
Theft and receipt ($50)	18/03/75	Idem	Case referred 23/05/75
Breaking and entering with intent	18/03/75	Idem	Case referred 23/05/75
Burglary and receipt	18/03/75	Idem	Case referred 23/05/75

Dossier No. 4 continued

Infractions Ascribed by the Social Welfare Court to the Delinquent prior to the Referral	Dates of Appearances	Decisions Made by the Social Welfare Court prior to the Referral	Infractions for which He Was Referred to Adult Court
Escape (from trade school)	18/03/75	Error in the dossier; deferred sine die.	
Burglary and receipt ($600)	18/03/75	Sine die because of preceding dossier.	
Burglary and receipt ($46)	24/03/75	Idem	
Possession of drugs	01/04/75	Idem	
Breaking and entering with intent	01/04/75	Idem	
Breaking and entering with intent	01/04/75	See above.	
Idem	Idem	Idem	
Idem	Idem	Idem	
Idem	Idem	Idem; 07/04/75, escapes again; summons issued; 10/04/75, taken to BF; 21/04/75, escapes from St. Vallier; summons issued; motion for referral on dossier of the theft and receipt ($150) dated 17/03/75 and subsequent dossiers; kept at St. Hyacinthe pending the decision on referral.	
Common assault	23/04/75	In view of the motion for referral, appearance postponed sine die.	
Armed robbery ($16,150)	23/04/75	Motion for referral accepted; at the request of the defence, the Superior Court orders the Social Welfare Court to hear a witness before deciding on referral, and to keep the child in an institution under the jurisdiction of the Social Welfare Court; detention at Berthelet; new referral 25/06/75.	Case referred 25/06/75

Indecent assault 23/04/75 Case referred 25/06/75

Breaking and entering 23/04/75 Case referred 25/06/75

Child's Attitude in Protective Environment

Preventive Detention

07/04/72 to 12/04/72 (age 14)
11/07/74 to 02/08/74 (age 16)

Report from Foster Homes

None

Report from Training Schools

Keeps bad company: he accompanies another youth in all the infractions.

Child's Family Situation

Father an alcoholic; works in Ontario; mother suffers from depression.

Child's School Situation

Frequent changes of school; absenteeism; behind in schooling.

Reasons for Referral to the Court of Sessions of the Peace

Previous escapes.
A dangerous person.
Little chance of rehabilitation.

Dossier No. 5

Date of Birth: August 10, 1958

Sex: Male

Infractions Ascribed by the Social Welfare Court to the Delinquent prior to the Referral	Dates of Appearances	Decisions Made by the Social Welfare Court prior to the Referral	Infractions for which He Was Referred to Adult Court
Theft and receipt	12/08/66 (age 8)	Adjourned sine die.	
Burglary and receipt	10/05/67	Adjourned sine die on parole; 10/08/67, good report from the PO; 11/01/68, goes to school regularly; 08/05/68, difficulties: reopening of the dossier (attempted housebreaking, falsification of the price of merchandise); detention at St. Vallier until 09/04/70; 09/04/70, returned to his mother.	
Burglary and receipt	21/05/70	Dossier adjourned to 12/06/70; 12/06/70, poor report from the PO; last change, if not, detention.	
Theft and receipt (bicycle)	21/05/70	Idem; 28/08/70, good report; suspension of final regulation.	
Theft and receipt (bicycle)	10/10/70	Order to behave; adjourned; 26/02/71, good report form the PO; goes to school; adjourned sine die.	
Attempt theft	18/05/71	Detention at St. Vallier until 30/06/71; 30/06/71, returned to his parents with recommendations; adjourned sine die.	
Theft and receipt ($1.40)	18/05/71	Idem	
Having stolen goods	09/08/71	Released (absence of the judge); 19/08/71, request for admission to Notre Dame de la Merci (Huberdeau); adjourned sine die.	

Offense	Date	Disposition
Theft and receipt ($100)	28/08/71	Detention at St. Vallier; 29/09/71, no room at Huberdeau; returned to his mother.
Theft and receipt ($25)	25/08/71	Idem
Burglary and receipt ($395)	25/08/71	Idem
Attempted breaking and entering with intent	25/10/71	Detention and clinical examination at Berthelet; 01/12/71, returned to his parents.
Burglary and receipt ($145)	15/12/71	Training Center until 31/01/72; 31/01/72, returned to his mother conditionally: regular interviews.
Attempted breaking and entering with intent	15/03/72	Detention until 26/04/72; 26/04/72, at Huberdeau; 02/05/72, back to court: does not conform to the requirements of Notre Dame de la Merci; detention.
Compound robbery (threats of violence; $4.30)	01/09/72	Detention; 05/09/72, returned to Huberdeau; 26/09/72, escapes from Huberdeau, comes back the same day; 04/05/73, escapes; 13/10/73, escapes.
Theft and receipt of auto	07/10/74	Detention until 31/10/74; 31/10/74, returned to his parents; request for admission to Mont St. Antoine.
	07/11/74	Detention at Berthelet because he broke his parole.
Burglary and receipt ($770)	13/11/74	Detention until 19/12/74; refuses to go to Mont St. Antoine; returned to his parents conditionally.
Compound robbery and (threats of violence; $3)	03/02/75	Admitted to Mont St. Antoine; adjourned sine die.
Theft and receipt ($80)	03/02/75	Idem
Lying drunk (municipal bylaw)	03/02/75	Idem

Dossier No. 5 continued

Infractions Ascribed by the Social Welfare Court to the Delinquent prior to the Referral	Dates of Appearances	Decisions Made by the Social Welfare Court prior to the Referral	Infractions for which He Was Referred to Adult Court
Theft and receipt of auto	28/04/75	Detention at St. Vallier; 04/05/75, escapes; summons to appear; 05/05/75, detention; 09/05/75, escapes; 26/05/75, prison at St. Hyacinthe until 11/06/75.	Case referred 07/07/75
Burglary and receipt ($400)	28/04/75	Idem; ran away from center; summons to appear.	Case referred 07/07/75
Burglary and receipt	28/04/75	Idem	Case referred 07/07/75
Theft and receipt ($1000)	28/04/75	Idem	Case referred 07/07/75
Burglary and receipt ($2,152)	28/04/75	Idem	Case referred 07/07/75
Burglary and receipt ($1,202)	28/04/75	Idem	Case referred 07/07/75
Theft and possession of auto	07/05/75	Idem	Case referred 07/07/75
Burglary and receipt ($400)	26/05/75	Idem	Case referred 07/07/75
Compound robbery ($1,039), revolver	04/07/75	11/06/75, request for referral; 12/06/75, escape from St. Vallier; 04/07/75, committed to Parthenais.	Case referred 07/07/75
Compound robbery ($63), sawed-off shotgun	04/07/75	Idem	Case referred 07/07/75
Compound robbery ($228), .22 revolver	04/07/75	Idem	Case referred 07/07/75

			Case referred 07/07/75
Compound robbery (imitation weapon)	04/07/75	Idem	Case referred 07/07/75
Burglary and receipt ($190)	04/07/75	Idem	Case referred 07/07/75
Burglary and receipt	04/07/75	Idem	Case referred 07/07/75

Child's Attitude in Protective Milieu

Report from Foster Homes	Report from Training Schools
None	Report from Berthelet 25/10/71: average intelligence, unstable, difficulty in controlling his impulses, no confirmed delinquent values, poor self-image.

Preventive Detention

11/02/70 to 09/03/70 (age 12)
02/05/72 to 05/09/72 (age 14)
07/11/74 to 19/12/74 (age 16)

Child's School Situation

Frequent changes of school; absenteeism; behind in schooling: in seventh grade at age 13.

Child's Family Situation

Mother alone; brothers and sisters at home.

Reasons for Referral to the Court of Sessions of the Peace

The court attempted rehabilitation at Huberdeau.
The child returned with numerous court records.
He escaped from Mont St. Antoine the very day he was placed there.
Further infractions.
More escapes from St. Vallier.
Impervious to rehabilitation of any kind.
The court had no further resources.

Dossier No. 6

Date of Birth: July 27, 1958

Sex: Male

Infractions Ascribed by the Social Welfare Court to the Delinquent prior to the Referral	Dates of Appearances	Decisions Made by the Social Welfare Court prior to the Referral	Infractions for which He Was Referred to Adult Court
Theft and receipt	07/07/72	Detention; adjourned sine die; escape from St. Vallier 29/07/72.	
Theft and possession of auto	30/08/72	Adjourned sine die; detention at St. Vallier; declared juvenile delinquent.	
Breaking and entering with intent	30/08/72	Idem	
		12/09/72, committed to Berthelet (rehabilitation) until 11/12/72; 23/09/72, escapes from Berthelet; summons to appear.	
Theft and possession of auto	04/10/72	Case adjourned sine die; return to Berthelet.	
		19/01/73, committed to Mont St. Antoine; escapes 22/01/73.	
Theft and possession of auto	31/01/73	Detention until 26/02/73; return to MSA; 26/02/73, detention, return 16/03/73 (age 15).	
		Numerous escapes; MSA no longer willing to take the child back; under detention; 12/04/73, under detention; 14/05/73, released conditionally (finds employment); 11/06/73, good report from PO: is working.	
Compound robbery ($92), knife	18/06/73	Adjourned sine die; detention	
Compound robbery ($73)	18/06/73	Adjourned sine die; detention at Berthelet; 24/06/73; escapes from Berthelet; summons; 29/06/73, summons canceled.	

Compound robbery ($26.80), violence or threats of	29/06/73	Case adjourned sine die.
Theft and possession of auto	29/06/73	Detention at Berthelet; 13/07/73; escapes; summons; 20/07/73, brought to court; detention, 26/07/73 until 31/10/73 (resocialization); 24/10/73, Boscoville for indefinite period; St. Vallier while waiting; 01/11/73, appearance before the court after having escaped; detention; 05/12/73, released conditionally: finds work; 28/01/74, adjourned sine die.
Theft and possession of auto	28/01/74	Under detention at St. Vallier; 29/01/74, escapes; summons.
Theft and possession of auto	28/01/74	Idem; trial sine die.
Theft and possession of auto	13/02/74	Idem; adjourned sine die in view of main dossier.
Theft and possession of auto	13/02/74	See above.
Compound robbery ($200), threats of violence or violence	13/02/74	Idem
Compound robbery	13/02/74	Main dossier; detention; 08/03/74, Berthelet for rehabilitation until 07/06/74; 07/06/74, report from Berthelet (see report from training schools); released on condition that he behave properly and work; adjourned sine die.
Theft and possession of auto and contents	14/08/74	Is working and already on probation; $25 fine or a week under detention; 28/11/74, brought to court on other charges; nonpayment of fine; recidivism; detention and psychiatric examination ordered.
Forgery and use of forgery	28/11/74	Detention; 06/12/74, released (at home, working).
Theft and possession of auto	28/11/74	Idem

Dossier No. 6 continued

Infractions Ascribed by the Social Welfare Court to the Delinquent prior to the Referral	Dates of Appearances	Decisions Made by the Social Welfare Court prior to the Referral	Infractions for which He Was Referred to Adult Court
Theft and possession of auto	16/01/75	Transfer warrant; 11/07/75, adjourned in order to find what measure to take; under detention at Berthelet.	Case referred 28/08/75
Compound robbery ($3,834), sawed-off .22 caliber rifle	11/07/75	Detention at Berthelet; 08/08/75, trial; 01/08/75, escapes; summons to appear; appears on warrant; because of escapes, is committed to adult prison until 22/08/75 at Cowansville; trial; hearing up to 28/08/75.	Case referred 28/08/75
Compound robbery ($2,338), sawed-off rifle	18/08/75	Idem	Case referred 28/08/75
Compound robbery ($1,076)	18/08/75	Idem	Case referred 28/08/75

Child's Attitude in Protective Milieu

Preventive Detention	Report from Foster Homes	Report from Training Schools
29/03/72 to 14/05/72 (age 14)	None	Report from Berthelet 03/01/73: no problem with groups; instability with regard to activities; manipulator. Report from Berthelet 07/06/74: considerable progress; intelligent; loses control, cannot accept defeat; instigator; no guilt feelings.

Child's Family Situation

Mother alone; father works in Sudbury, Ontario.

Child's School Situation

In 1972, in eighth grade at age 13.

Academic activities: alert mind, mentally lazy, participation good. Not rehabilitated, but stay profitable.

Reasons for Transfer to the Court of Sessions of the Peace

Failure to rehabilitate.
Nature and gravity of the infractions.
Psychiatric report: delinquent child, no motivation for protective rehabilitation.

Dossier No. 7

Date of Birth: January 22, 1958

Sex: Male

Infractions Ascribed by the Social Welfare Court to the Delinquent prior to the Referral	Dates of Appearances	Decisions Made by the Social Welfare Court prior to the Referral	Infractions for which He Was Referred to Adult Court
Damage to property	24/03/70	Adjourned sine die.	
		Petition under article 15 (July 7), hearing 17/07/70; under detention until the 24/07/70, when child returned to his mother; child promises to behave; on probation.	
		14/09/70, child involves young brother in drugs; under detention; clinical examination ordered.	
		24/10/70, referred to SSSF, Mount Royal Branch; released on parole.	
		24/11/70, order for detention at St. Vallier (is making trouble at home).	
		04/12/70, under detention until 05/02/71 (father away, mother ill).	
		05/02/71, father returns; released; 22/04/71, good report from PO.	
		16/11/71, under detention (mother asks for child's placement because she is alone).	
		16/12/71, PO asks for placement at Notre Dame de la Merci (Huberdeau).	
		24/01/72, mother asks that child be returned.	
		05/07/72, under detention because mother in hospital.	

Charge	Date	Disposition
		06/07/72, PO is on holiday; adjourned until 20/07/72 (under detention at Berthelet).
		20/07/72, under detention until 21/08/72 while awaiting placement in foster home.
		28/08/72, escapes from Berthelet; order for transfer.
		21/09/72, warrant canceled; foster home found; mother insists on taking child back; returns home; adjourned sine die.
		10/04/73, investigation of the children in the family under article 15.
		25/04/73, court takes the child under its protection and orders clinical reevaluation; detention for observation in closed clinical milieu until 28/05/73.
		28/05/73, committed to Mont St. Antoine; escapes from court; summons issued.
		17/07/73 to 17/10/73, detention at Berthelet; 17/10/73, judge absent; detention until 22/10/73.
		22/10/73, child refused admission to Mont St. Antoine; returned to mother; on probation.
Burglary and receipt	19/12/73	Detention.
Theft and receipt ($200)	12/02/74	Periodically adjourned until 22/08/74; 22/08/74, father returns home; children well controlled; court adjourns case sine die.
Compound robbery and theft of auto ($500)	16/09/74	Under detention until 30/09/74 (trial) at Youth Training Center; 04/10/74, adjourned sine die; returns to family on probation; 06/11/74, dossier reopened; detention at St. Vallier; 07/11/74, escapes; summons issued; petition for referral despite request of the defense to make new representations; request refused.
		Case referred to adult court on charge of compound robbery and theft of automobile (first appearance September 16, 1974).

Dossier No. 7 continued

Infractions Ascribed by the Social Welfare Court to the Delinquent prior to the Referral	Dates of Appearances	Decisions Made by the Social Welfare Court prior to the Referral	Infractions for which He Was Referred to Adult Court
Compound robbery ($200)	16/09/74	Idem	Case referred 11/11/74
Compound robbery ($830)	16/09/74	Idem	Case referred 11/11/74
Compound robbery ($15)	16/09/74	Idem; 19/11/74, detention at Parthenais.	
Compound robbery ($65)	27/11/74	Referred.	Case referred 27/11/74
		05/12/74, the Court of Sessions rejects referrals of November 11 for violation of the rule "audi alteram partem"; orders that the child be placed in a center for children; 28/01/75, Boscoville; 30/01/75, escapes; 06/02/75, apprehended; detention St. Vallier; escape.	
Theft and possession of auto	23/12/74	10/03/75, case referred; Parthenais	Case referred 10/03/75
Burglary and receipt ($1,350)	23/12/75	Idem	Case referred 10/03/75
Compound robbery ($100), starting-pistol	23/12/75	Idem	Case referred 10/03/75
Compound robbery ($100), starting-pistol	23/12/75	Idem	Case referred 10/03/75
Theft and possession of automobile	23/12/75	Idem	Case referred 10/03/75
Compound robbery ($1,000), starting-pistol	23/12/75	Idem	Case referred 10/03/75

Compound robbery ($20)	23/12/75	Idem	Case referred 10/03/75
Compound robbery	23/12/75	Idem	Case referred 10/03/75
Theft and possession of auto	23/12/75	Idem	Case referred 10/03/75
Theft and possession of auto	23/12/75	Idem	Case referred 10/03/75
Attempted breaking and entering with intent	05/02/75	Idem	Case referred 10/03/75
Compound robbery ($200), crowbar	06/02/75	Idem	Case referred 10/03/75

Preventive detention	*Report from Foster Homes*	*Child's Attitude in Protective Milieu*	*Report from Training Schools*
17/07/70 to 24/07/70	None		None
24/11/70 to 05/02/71	None		None
16/11/71 to 24/01/72	None		None
05/07/72 to 28/08/72	None		None

Child's Family Situation

Father a criminal, often in prison; mother sometimes practices prostitution.

Child's School Situation

Frequent changes of school; absenteeism; behind in schooling; repeated fifth grade three times, with very little progress.

Reasons for Referral to the Court of Sessions of the Peace

Age of the delinquent.
No motivation to become resocialized.
Refusal to follow treatment.
The child in danger.
Recommendation of 2 years' stay at St. Vincent de Paul to learn a trade.
Numerous past and continuing offences.

Dossier No. 8

Date of Birth: April 21, 1957

Sex: Male

Infractions Ascribed by the Social Welfare Court to the Delinquent prior to the Referral	Dates of Appearances	Decisions Made by the Social Welfare Court prior to the Referral	Infractions for which He Was Referred to Adult Court
Disturbing the peace	21/09/72 (age 15)	Adjourned sine die.	
Disturbing the peace	06/10/72	Adjourned sine die.	
Attempted theft of auto	13/04/73	Adjourned sine die; preventive detention until 24/04/73.	
Compound robbery ($5)	23/07/73	Detention Berthelet Center from 30/08/73 to 27/11/73 (age 16).	
Possession of arms with dangerous intent	27/07/73	Adjourned sine die in view of detention.	
Compound robbery and assault and battery ($110)	22/04/74	Adjourned sine die.	
Assault against constable	08/08/74	Failure to appear; adjourned sine die.	
Conspiracy and armed robbery, two thefts ($3 and $120), sawed-off rifle	29/08/74	Adjourned sine die; detention at St. Vallier (age 17).	
Conspiracy and compound robbery ($250), revolver	29/08/74	Sine die; see above.	
Possession of restricted arms	29/08/74	Sine die; see above.	
Burglary and receipt ($10)	29/08/74	Idem	
Conspiracy for armed robbery	29/08/74	Idem	

Offence	Date	Outcome	
Possession of arms with dangerous intent (.22 caliber sawed-off shotgun)	13/11/74	Petition for referral; will be detained at St. Hyacinthe	Case referred
Compound robbery ($350), weapon offence	14/01/75	Action rejected.	
Armed robbery	14/01/75	Petition for referral; prisoner at St. Hyacinthe.	Case referred
Attempted murder	14/01/75	Idem	Case referred
Compound robbery	14/01/75	Idem	Case referred

Child's Attitude in Protective Milieu

Report from Foster Homes	Report from Training Schools
None	None

Preventive Detention

13/04/73 to 24/04/73 (age 16): parents away, grandmother incapable of looking after him.

20/08/73 to 27/11/73 (age 16)

22/03/74 to ?/11/74: 3 admissions to St. Vallier.

26/11/74: St. Hyacinthe.

Child's School Situation

Does not attend school; works; is at about tenth grade level.

Child's Family Situation

Father at Manic 5; three sisters; four brothers; drug problem.

Reasons for Referral to the Court of Sessions of the Peace

In view of his age, his crimes, and the gravity of the offences, even Boscoville had no success. Prognosis poor. Does not admit the need to be helped.

Dossier No. 9

Date of Birth: September 20, 1957

Sex: Male

Infractions Ascribed by the Social Welfare Court to the Delinquent prior to the Referral	Dates of Appearances	Decisions Made by the Social Welfare Court prior to the Referral	Infractions for which He Was Referred to Adult Court
	19/11/73	Request for protection under article 15: child uncontrollable, does not go to school, takes drugs; detention; 14/12/73, released on parole; on probation; adjourned sine die.	
Burglary ($40)	07/01/74	Psychiatric examination ordered; adjourned sine dine.	
Burglary and receipt ($1,840)	01/08/74	Adjourned sine die (age 17).	
Burglary and receipt ($435)	01/08/74	Adjourned sine die.	
Breaking and entering with intent	01/08/74	Adjourned sine die.	
Theft and receipt of auto	15/10/74	Adjourned sine die.	
Theft and receipt of auto	15/10/74	Adjourned sine die.	
Theft and receipt of auto	15/10/74	Adjourned sine die.	
Theft and receipt of auto	15/10/74	Adjourned sine die; placed in Mont St. Antoine in December 1974; escape from Mont St. Antoine 06/01/75; commits theft 17/01/75; returned by police to Mont St. Antoine 18/01/75.	
Theft of auto	23/01/75	Psychiatric evaluation ordered; detention at Berthelet while awaiting return to Mont St. Antoine; 24/02/75, escapes from MSA on day of arrival; 25/02/75, court annuls placement at MSA (cont.)	

Possession of imitation weapon (sawed-off .303 caliber shotgun)	21/03/75	Detention; motion for referral accepted.	Case referred 21/03/75
Compound robbery ($1,675)	21/03/75	Idem	Case referred 21/03/75
Injury with intent	13/05/75	Idem	Case referred 15/05/75
Burglary and receipt ($900)	20/06/75	Idem	Case referred 23/06/75

Child's Attitude in Protective Milieu

Report from Foster Homes	Report from Training Schools
None	None

Preventive Detention

19/11/73 to 14/12/73 (age 16)

Child's School Situation

Frequent changes of school; absenteeism; behind in schooling; repeated first grade three times; repeated fourth grade twice; poor marks; left school at age 15.

Child's Family Situation

Mother alone; three brothers and five sisters at home.

Reasons for Referral to the Court of Sessions of the Peace

The large number of crimes.
The lack of institutions able to answer his needs.
Will be 18 years old 20/09/75.
The court had no further resources.

Dossier No. 10

Date of Birth: July 6, 1957

Sex: Male

Infractions Ascribed by the Social Welfare Court to the Delinquent prior to the Referral	Dates of Appearances	Decisions Made by the Social Welfare Court prior to the Referral	Infractions for which He Was Referred to Adult Court
Immoral conduct	09/09/71	On probation; adjourned sine die.	
Damages ($34.10)	30/09/71 (age 14)	Sine die.	
Burglary and receipt ($1,030)	09/12/71	Detention until 17/12/71; 17/12/71 sine die.	
Burglary and receipt ($590)	09/12/71	Idem	
Burglary and receipt ($1,484)	09/12/71	Idem	
Burglary and receipt ($74)	09/12/71	Idem	
Attempted breaking and entering	09/12/71	Idem	
Burglary and receipt ($250)	09/12/71	Idem	
Burglary and receipt ($182)	09/12/71	Idem	
Burglary and receipt ($800)	09/12/71	Idem	
Burglary and receipt ($4,584)	09/12/71	Idem; 10/01/72, entrusted to the care of child's uncle; 07/02/72, good report from PO; goes to school regularly; 27/07/72, adjourned sine die.	

Offense	Date	Disposition
Immoral conduct	05/06/72	Declared juvenile delinquent; on probation of the Sun Youth Organization; 27/07/72, adjourned sine die; work of the PO continued.
Municipal bylaw	26/07/72	Reprimand by the court; child already on probation; 09/11/72, adjourned sine die.
Burglary and receipt	06/09/74	Case dismissed: insufficient proof (age 17).
Breaking and entering with intent	27/01/75	Already under the supervision of Sun Youth; sentence suspended.
Burglary and receipt	27/02/75	Detention at Berthelet; 11/04/75, adjourned sine die.
Burglary and receipt ($200)	21/03/75	Idem
Burglary and receipt ($1,700)	21/03/75	Idem
Burglary and receipt ($600)	21/03/75	Idem
Burglary and receipt ($407)	21/03/75	Idem
Burglary and receipt ($133)	21/03/75	Idem
Burglary and receipt ($2,400)	21/03/75	Idem
Burglary and receipt ($650)	21/03/75	Idem
Burglary and receipt ($3,500)	21/03/75	Idem
Burglary and receipt ($1,000)	21/03/75	Idem

Dossier No. 10 continued

Infractions Ascribed by the Social Welfare Court to the Delinquent prior to the Referral	Dates of Appearances	Decisions Made by the Social Welfare Court prior to the Referral	Infractions for which He Was Referred to Adult Court
Theft and receipt of auto	21/03/75	Idem	
Burglary and receipt ($2,320)	21/03/75	Idem	
Burglary and receipt ($914)	21/03/75	Idem	
Burglary and receipt ($8,800)	01/04/75	Clinical examination ordered; detention until 05/05/75; released on parole; 29/05/75, request for referral.	Case referred 29/05/75
Burglary and receipt ($200)	01/04/75	Idem	Case referred 29/05/75
Burglary and receipt ($3,685)	01/04/75	Idem	Case referred 29/05/75
Burglary and receipt ($3,445)	01/04/75	Idem	Case referred 29/05/75
Burglary and receipt ($1,450)	01/04/75	Idem	Case referred 29/05/75
Burglary and receipt ($1,500)	01/04/75	Idem	Case referred 29/05/75
Burglary and receipt ($200)	01/04/75	Idem	Case referred 29/05/75
Burglary and receipt ($3,015)	01/04/75	Idem	Case referred 29/05/75
Burglary and receipt ($1,940)	01/04/75	Idem	Case referred 29/05/75

Burglary and receipt ($1,550)	01/04/75	Idem	Case referred 29/05/75
Burglary and receipt ($235)	01/04/75	Idem	Case referred 29/05/75
Burglary and receipt ($200)	01/04/75	Idem	Case referred 29/05/75

Child's Attitude in Protective Milieu

Preventive Detention	*Report from Foster Homes*	*Report from Training Schools*
None	None	None

Child's Family Situation

Child's School Situation

Father and mother; one sister and two brothers at home.

Frequent changes of school; absenteeism; behind in schooling.

Reasons for Referral to the Court of Sessions of the Peace

The court had no more resources with which to help the child.
Gravity and number of crimes.
The interest of both the child and society.

Dossier No. 11

Date of Birth: January 22, 1957

Sex: Male

Infractions Ascribed by the Social Welfare Court to the Delinquent prior to the Referral	Dates of Appearances	Decisions Made by the Social Welfare Court prior to the Referral	Infractions for which He Was Referred to Adult Court
	14/02/66 (age 9)	Request for protection under article 15 (child continually running away from home and showing predelinquent characteristics); psychiatric examination ordered; probation; February 1966 to April 1968, regular interviews; under the protection of the Society for the Protection of Women and Children; 08/04/68, entrusted to the care of his grandmother in Ontario; 05/04/71, returns to his parents; 11/11/71, does not respond to appeal; is returned to his grandmother (Cote St. Luc).	
Burglary and receipt ($600)	31/08/72	Detention; adjourned until 08/09/72, when adjourned sine die; entrusted to his father's care (age 15); clinical examination September 18.	
Theft and receipt of bicycle	31/08/72	Idem	
Loafing and prowling the streets at night	10/10/72	Declared juvenile delinquent; entrusted to his grandmother's care; ordered by the court to either attend school or find a job; 17/11/72, behavior satisfactory; Does not want to return to school; 04/12/72, has a job; grandmother assigned as foster home; 13/12/72, returns to his father's home; placed in charge of Children's Service, which supervises the foster home of the grandmother.	

Theft and receipt of auto	29/08/73	Detention until 04/09/73; 05/09/73, entrusted to father's care; has to see his probation officer once a week; clinical examination ordered; 13 and 19/09/73, examination; 20/09/73, ordered to appear; 24/09/73, adjourned sine die.
Breaking and entering	24/09/73	Detention until 09/10/73; placement at Boys' Farm and Training School considered; Detention until 22/10/73; 22/10/73, placed with grandmother while waiting for Boys' Farm; 29/10/73, runs away from grandmother's home; ordered to appear; 04/01/74, summons annulled; detention; 21/01/74, adjourned sine die.
Attempted compound robbery	07/01/74	Complaint dismissed.
Compound robbery ($100)	07/01/74	Trial adjourned sine die.
Compound robbery ($6)	07/01/74	Detention until 23/01/74; 23/01/74, taken to Boys' Farm.
Compound robbery	07/01/74	Benefit of the doubt; insufficient evidence; sine die.
Theft and receipt of auto	25/01/74	Appearance adjourned sine die because he is at the Boys' Farm; 28/01/74, move to have him referred under consideration: adjourned to 08/03/74.
Attempted theft	25/01/74	Idem
Theft and receipt ($125)	25/01/74	Idem
Theft and receipt of auto	28/01/74	Idem
Theft and receipt of auto	28/01/74	Idem; 30/01/74, escapes from St. Vallier; warrant; returns of his own accord 01/02/74; detention until 25/02/74; 06/02/74, escapes from St. Vallier; warrant; annulled 28/02/74.

Dossier No. 11 continued

Infractions Ascribed by the Social Welfare Court to the Delinquent prior to the Referral	Dates of Appearances	Decisions Made by the Social Welfare Court prior to the Referral	Infractions for which He Was Referred to Adult Court
Theft and receipt of vehicle	28/02/74	Appearance before the court; detention at Parthenais; motion for referral.	
Burglary and receipt ($150)	08/03/74	Adjourned until 11/03/74; 11/03/74, judgment on the motion at Boys' Farm.	
Attempted breaking and entering	08/03/74	Idem	
Breaking and entering with intent	08/03/74	Idem	
Burglary and receipt ($245)	08/03/74	Idem	
Burglary and receipt ($79)	08/03/74	Idem	
Breaking and entering with intent	08/03/74	Idem	
Theft and receipt of auto	08/03/74	Idem; 22/05/74, runs away from home; warrant; 30/05/74, returned to Boys' Farm; 16/06/74, escapes from BF; warrant; 25/06/74, detention until 03/07/74 at the request of the BF; 28/06/74, BF until 10/07/74; 23/08/74, escapes from BF; 13/09/74, adjourned sine die.	
Burglary and receipt ($100)	13/09/74	Appearance deferred until 20/09/74; detention; 20/09/74, motion for referral; detention.	Case referred 09/12/74
Theft and receipt ($200)	13/09/74	See above.	Case referred 09/12/74
Burglary and receipt ($20)	13/09/74	Idem	Case referred 09/12/74

Compound robbery ($7,000)	02/12/74	Idem	Case referred 09/12/74
Receiving	02/12/74	Idem	Case referred 09/12/74
Theft and receipt of auto	02/12/74	Idem	Case referred 09/12/74

Child's Attitude in Protective Milieu

Report from Foster Homes	Report from Training Schools
None	Child passive; very depressive; normal intelligence; vindictive behavior; under the influence of a friend and follows him in all his projects.

Preventive Detention

04/01/74 to 23/01/74 (age 17)
25/06/74 to 28/06/74

Child's School Situation

Frequent changes of school; absenteeism; behind in his schooling.

Child's Family Situation

Father an alcoholic; mother a diabetic and hostile to the children; two brothers, one in institution at Shawbridge; family milieu very poor.

Reasons for Referral to the Court of Sessions of the Peace

Is not willing to accept the help of the court.
Good of the child.
The good of society.

Dossier No. 12

Date of Birth: January 3, 1957

Sex: Male

Infractions Ascribed by the Social Welfare Court to the Delinquent prior to the Referral	Dates of Appearances	Decisions Made by the Social Welfare Court prior to the Referral	Infractions for which He Was Referred to Adult Court
Attempted breaking and entering with intent	05/03/70 (age 13)	Declared juvenile delinquent; issue adjourned sine die; released on parole.	
Attempted theft	23/03/70	Detention till 28/03/70; 28/03/70, adjourned sine die.	
Theft and receipt ($180)	23/03/70	Idem	
Theft and receipt ($88)	21/09/70	Action dismissed.	
Theft and receipt of bicycle	30/09/70	Detention at St. Vallier until 14/10/70; 14/10/70, declared juvenile delinquent; handed over to the parents to be sent to the country in care of his grandparents; 11/12/70, good report; 04/08/70, adjourned sine die.	
Theft and receipt of auto	29/12/70	Appearance adjourned; 04/01/71, appeared, released; 03/02/71, refused at Mont St. Antoine in view of his age (13); 04/08/71, adjourned sine die.	
Burglary and receipt ($400)	12/03/71	Request for admission to Quatre Vents; released on parole on condition he leave his gang; 04/08/71, adjourned.	
Burglary and receipt ($372)	05/05/71	Detention at St. Vallier (sniffing glue and associating with his gang); 09/05/71, escapes from St. Vallier; warrant issued 17/05/71; 04/08/71, adjourned.	

Offence	Date	Disposition
Burglary and receipt ($584)	05/05/71	Idem
Theft and receipt of auto	17/05/71	Detention at Berthelet until 04/08/71; 04/08/71, at home; 27/09/71, adjourned sine die.
Burglary and receipt ($85)	08/09/71	Appearance adjourned; 13/09/71, appearance on a new offence; 27/09/71, declared juvenile delinquent; adjourned sine die.
Theft and receipt of bicycle	08/09/71	Idem
Theft and receipt of auto	13/09/71	Detention until 02/11/71; admission to Mont St. Antoine; 19/11/71, escapes from MSA; returned 21/11/71; 29/11/71, escapes from MSA; will return 15/06/72; runs away the same day.
Theft and receipt of auto	15/05/72	Detention at Berthelet; back to MSA 15/06/72; 15/06/72, runs away from MSA; warrant ordered; 01/08/72, adjourned sine die.
Attempted theft of auto	01/08/72	Detention until 15/08/72; 15/08/72, Mont St. Antoine; 12/09/72, escapes, warrant; 04/06/73, adjourned sine die.
Theft and receipt of auto	27/10/72	Detention until 31/10/72; 31/10/72, released on probation (age 15) on condition he go to school; placement at MSA rescinded; adjourned sine die.
Breaking and entering with intent	20/12/72	Released on parole; 08/01/73, adjourned; 04/06/73, adjourned sine die.
Attempted auto theft	03/01/73	Detention until 08/01/73, then released on parole; 04/06/73, complaint dismissed because the victim and witnesses failed to appear.
Breaking and entering with intent	19/03/73	Detention St. Vallier; 06/04/73, warrant; 04/06/73, adjourned sine die.

Dossier No. 12 continued

Infractions Ascribed by the Social Welfare Court to the Delinquent prior to the Referral	Dates of Appearances	Decisions Made by the Social Welfare Court prior to the Referral	Infractions for which He Was Referred to Adult Court
Theft and receipt of auto	19/07/73	Child injured; appearance adjourned until 10/09/73; released on parole; September 1973, working at Joliette; good at his work; $10 fine or a week in detention by 11/09/73; fine paid; adjourned sine die.	
Theft and receipt of auto	16/10/73	Trial set for 05/12/73; does not appear; summons; 21/02/74, brought to court; detention until 13/03/74; 13/03/74, trial; detention at Berthelet; 14/03/74, escapes; warrant; 17/07/74, adjourned sine die.	
Theft and receipt of auto	23/04/74	Detention; 03/05/74, escapes; warrant; 27/06/74, detention in view of his age, his escapes, his many previous offences; 07/05/74, detention; 17/07/74, adjourned sine die.	
Theft and receipt of truck	13/05/74	Adjourned to 27/06/74; 27/06/74, has a job; promise to appear 17/07/74; released; turned out of the house; 17/07/74, adjourned sine die.	
Lying drunk (municipal bylaw)	25/07/74	Failure to appear; 01/08/74, despite notice, does not appear; summons; 15/11/74, adjourned on decision to refer.	
Compound robbery (revolver)	30/08/74	Warrant for committal at Parthenais; hearing of the motion for referral 27/09/74; under observation at l'Institut Pinel; decision on referral postponed to 11/02/75.	Case referred 11/02/75
Conspiracy	30/08/74	Idem	Case referred 11/02/75
Attempted compound robbery	30/08/74	Idem	Case referred 11/02/75

Offense	Date	Status	Referral
Conspiracy	30/08/74	Idem	Case referred 11/02/75
Conspiracy and attempted auto theft	29/11/74	16/12/74, order for committal to Parthenais with instructions to take him to Pinel; report from Pinel postponed to 11/02/75 because the youth had to change psychiatrists.	Case referred 11/02/75
Conspiracy	24/08/74	Idem	Case referred 11/02/75
Burglary and receipt ($2,000)	27/08/74	See above.	Case referred 11/02/75
Conspiracy to commit compound robbery ($190), revolver	27/08/74	Idem	Case referred 11/02/75
Conspiracy, kidnapping, and illegal restraint ($200), sawed-off shotgun	27/08/74	Idem	Case referred 11/02/75
Idem	27/08/74	Idem	Case referred 11/02/75
Conspiracy for compound robbery ($1,260), sawed-off shotgun	27/08/74	Idem	Case referred 11/02/75
Conspiracy and compound robbery	27/08/74	Idem	Case referred 11/02/75
Conspiracy and compound robbery ($150), revolver	27/08/74	Idem	Case referred 11/02/75
Conspiracy for compound robbery and sequestration (auto) (revolver)	27/08/74	Idem	Case referred 11/02/75
Idem ($189), revolver	27/08/74	Idem	Case referred 11/02/75
Conspiracy and compound robbery ($300), revolver	27/08/74	Idem	Case referred 11/02/75
Conspiracy and attempted compound robbery (pistol)	27/08/74	Idem	Case referred 11/02/75

Dossier No. 12 continued

Infractions Ascribed by the Social Welfare Court to the Delinquent prior to the Referral	Dates of Appearances	Decisions Made by the Social Welfare Court prior to the Referral	Infractions for which He Was Referred to Adult Court
Theft and receipt (two license plates)	27/08/74	Idem	Case referred 11/02/75
Burglary and receipt ($1,200)	27/08/74	Idem	Case referred 11/02/75
Conspiracy for compound robbery ($50), sawed-off shotgun and revolver	27/08/74	Idem	Case referred 11/02/75
Compound robbery ($33), sawed-off shotgun	27/08/74	Idem; 11/02/75, had to return to Parthenais because behavior unacceptable at Pinel.	Case referred 11/02/75

Preventive Detention	Report from Foster Homes	*Child's Attitude in Protective Milieu* Report from Training Schools
None	None	None

Child's School Situation

Frequent changes of school; absenteeism; behind in his schooling; In ninth grade at 15 years of age.

Child's Family Situation

Mother and father at home; father an alcoholic and a criminal; two sisters.

Reasons for Referral to the Court of Sessions of the Peace

All resources of the court had been tried.
Was 18 years old on 03/01/75.
Gravity and number of crimes.
Clinical report from the Institut Pinel.
Clinical report of the Children and Family Clinic, dating from 01/07/74: inveterate alcoholic; drug dependency since the age of 11 or 12 (in 1974, several admissions to hospital for this); total failure of all measures taken by the court; crimes more and more dangerous to society; persistence of hallucinatory syndrome (approaching delirium tremens); keeps away from all human contact; placed on observation for mental disorders.

Dossier No. 13

Date of Birth: December 28, 1956
Sex: Male

Infractions Ascribed by the Social Welfare Court to the Delinquent prior to the Referral	Dates of Appearances	Decisions Made by the Social Welfare Court prior to the Referral	Infractions for which He Was Referred to Adult Court
Burglary and receipt ($40)	11/10/68 (age 12)	First offence; adjourned sine die.	
Damage ($5,000)	13/05/69	Declared juvenile delinquent; adjourned sine die.	
Burglary and receipt ($15)	30/05/69	Idem	
Theft and receipt of bicycle	10/07/69	Adjourned sine die in view of the explanation given by the child.	
Attempted theft of contents of auto	10/10/69	Adjourned sine die; probation.	
Burglary and receipt ($38)	31/03/70	Mother had difficulty with the child; detention until 28/04/70 prior to appearing before the judge in possession of his dossier; 28/04/70, adjourned sine die since he was already under supervision of the court.	
Burglary and receipt	23/07/70	Detention; adjourned until 28/07/70; 28/07/70, returned home; sine die.	
Burglary and receipt	11/08/70	Detention St. Vallier; psychiatric examination ordered.	
Damage ($43)	01/10/70	Adjourned sine die; 20/10/70, released on probation.	

Dossier No. 13 continued

Infractions Ascribed by the Social Welfare Court to the Delinquent prior to the Referral	Dates of Appearances	Decisions Made by the Social Welfare Court prior to the Referral	Infractions for which He Was Referred to Adult Court
Burglary and receipt ($1,400)	27/11/70	Sine die; already on probation; 15/12/70, probation; good report from PO.	
Burglary and receipt ($150)	26/03/71	Sine die; already on probation.	
Burglary and receipt ($900)	13/04/71	Detention at St. Vallier; 23/04/71, released for surgery.	
Damage ($300)	20/04/71	Detention: see above; 14/06/71, declared juvenile delinquent; released on probation; sine die.	
Burglary and receipt ($3,000)	09/08/71	Placed 18/08/71 at Mont St. Antoine for undetermined period (age 15); 29/10/71, escapes; returned 02/11/71 by the court; escapes same day; returned by the court 24/11/71; 24/12/71, escapes; returns with his father 11/01/71; left 18/01/72.	
Breaking and entering with intent	26/01/72	Detention; 07/02/72, child given benefit of the doubt; 23/02/72, order for placement at MSA annulled; child not motivated; returned to his family conditionally; 14/03/72, good report from school.	
Loitering while drunk	31/05/72	Released on parole in care of parents; adjourned sine die.	
Theft and receipt of auto	21/06/72	Detention until 18/09/72; rehabilitation at Berthelet.	
Breaking and entering	05/07/72	Adjourned sine die; detention.	
Possession of tools for breaking in	05/07/72	Adjourned sine die; detention.	

Compound robbery	13/07/72	Adjourned sine die; detention; 18/09/72, promise to behave; released; 17/11/72, parents separated; leaves his mother to go with his father; conduct good.	
Not paying his fare on the metro	10/07/73	Fine of $5 payable in 15 days; in default of which a week in detention; 17/08/72, court strongly suggests he find a job.	
Burglary and receipt ($10)	27/08/73	Detention until 14/09/73; 14/09/73, returns to his mother on probation; adjourned sine die.	
Theft and receipt ($47.50)	24/04/74	Detention until 06/05/74; motion for referral; 17/07/74, referred; detention at Parthenais.	Case referred 17/07/74
Burglary and receipt ($10,000)	06/02/74	17/07/74, referred.	Case referred 17/07/74
Driving a car without a license	09/05/74	Idem	Case referred 17/07/74
Compound robbery ($59), threats of violence	12/07/74	Idem	Case referred 17/07/74
Burglary and receipt ($435)	12/07/74	Idem	Case referred 17/07/74
Burglary and receipt ($104)	14/08/74	14/08/74, referred.	Case referred 14/08/74
Burglary and receipt ($100)	14/08/74	Idem	Case referred 14/08/74
Attempted breaking and entering	14/08/74	Idem	Case referred 14/08/74
Burglary and receipt	14/08/74	Idem	Case referred 14/08/74
Breaks parole (is home between 1 P.M. and 6 P.M.)	14/03/74	Idem	Case referred 14/08/74
Possession of tools for breaking in	14/08/74	Idem	Case referred 14/08/74

Dossier No. 13 continued

Infractions Ascribed by the Social Welfare Court to the Delinquent prior to the Referral	Dates of Appearances	Decisions Made by the Social Welfare Court prior to the Referral	Infractions for which He Was Referred to Adult Court
Burglary and receipt ($1,000)	14/08/74	Idem	Case referred 14/08/74
Breaking and entering with intent	14/08/74	Idem	Case referred 14/08/74
Burglary and receipt ($900)			
Possession of tools for breaking in	27/09/74	27/09/74, referred.	Case referred 27/09/74
Burglary and receipt ($100)	27/09/74	Idem	Case referred 27/09/74
Burglary and receipt ($950)	27/09/74	Idem	Case referred 27/09/74
Theft with violence ($70)	07/10/74	Referred.	Case referred 07/10/74

Child's Attitude in Protective Milieu		
Preventive Detention	Report from Foster Homes	Report from Training Schools
31/03/70 to 28/05/70 (age 14)	None	None

Child's School Situation

Not very much behind in school; no failures.

Child's Family Situation

Three brothers and three sisters at home.

Reasons for Referral to the Court of Sessions of the Peace

In view of the crimes (indictable offences).
In view of his age (17 years).
Since all attempts to rehabilitate him had failed, it was decided to refer him to an adult court.

Dossier No. 14

Date of Birth: December 16, 1956

Sex: Male

Infractions Ascribed by the Social Welfare Court to the Delinquent prior to the Referral	Dates of Appearances	Decisions Made by the Social Welfare Court prior to the Referral	Infractions for which He Was Referred to Adult Court
	30/06/67 (age 11)	Mother in detention for abandonment; child placed at St. Vallier (art. 15): 10/08/67, first foster home; December 1968, the court orders a clinical examination; child placed in a children's center, l'Accueil des Jeunes; February 1969, second foster home; August 1969, St. Vallier; 02/09/69, Ecole Notre Dame de la Merci; 03/12/69, placement continued; 08/06/70, idem; 30/07/70 to 08/08/70, vacation at third foster home; 08/09/70, returned to Notre Dame de la Merci; beginning of 1971, steps to have the child adoptable; 18/06/71, third foster home (Mont St. Antoine home); 30/08/71, fourth foster home; 13/01/72, runs away from foster home; order to appear.	
	29/11/72	Appearance; child hidden by his mother; Berthelet Center; 17/01/73, admission to Mont St. Antoine (observation center); 20/03/73, Berthelet Center.	
Theft and receipt ($60)	14/05/73	Declared juvenile delinquent; Berthelet Center until June 1973 while waiting for admission to Boscoville; 30/07/73, vacation with his mother until 04/09/73 on condition he fulfill his obligations; 11/09/73, placement at Mont St. Antoine annulled at the request of the child; detention while awaiting admission to Boscoville; 24/09/73, order to appear before the judge.	

Dossier No. 14 continued

Infractions Ascribed by the Social Welfare Court to the Delinquent prior to the Referral	Dates of Appearances	Decisions Made by the Social Welfare Court prior to the Referral	Infractions for which He Was Referred to Adult Court
	25/11/73	Detention; 07/12/73, placement at Boscoville; 08/02/74, request for referral.	Case referred 15/11/74
Theft and receipt (three credit cards from an auto)	13/11/74	New referral, taken before the Court of Sessions.	Case referred 15/11/74
Theft and receipt of auto	13/11/74	Idem	Case referred 15/11/74

Child's Attitude in Protective Milieu

Preventive Detention	Report from Foster Homes	Report from Training Schools
None	10/08/67, first foster home, child behaving well; In June 1968, the mother is allowed to visit but not take the child out; 18/12/68, the child is expelled from school, and the home refuses to keep him.	December and January 1969, a month and a half at the Accueil des Jeunes.
	February 1969, second foster home; August 1969, trouble in the home: disreputable friends, refuses to be disciplined, wants to do as he pleases; home refuses to keep the child any longer.	
	30/07/70 to 08/09/70, vacation at third foster home.	August 29, St. Vallier; 02/09/69 to 30/07/70, Notre Dame de la Merci; 08/09/70, return to Notre Dame de la Merci.

18/06/71, third foster home (home of Mont St. Antoine); 10/01/72, good report; change of foster home: bad behavior; 06/06/72, won't accept the demands of the home; 13/10/72, runs away.

29/11/72, Berthelet Center; 17/01/73, Mont St. Antoine; several escapes; 20/03/73, Berthelet; 06/04/73, escapes; returned to Berthelet 14/05/73; 07/12/73, Boscoville; 15/01/74, escapes.

Child's School Situation

Frequent changes of school; absenteeism; behind in schooling; 18/12/68, sent back to school; put in grade usual for his age; did not repeat a year; between the age of 8 and 9, missed a year; in general, failures everywhere; refusal to attend school after being in foster home for some time.

Child's Family Situation

Mother alone; brothers and sisters at home; father unknown; unmarried mother unable to look after her children (several times in detention); adoptive parents deceased; a half-brother.

On the basis of these fourteen cases transferred by the juvenile court to the adult court, several remarks are in order. First of all, there are three denominators common to all these youths. They generally appeared in juvenile court for the first time under the Youth Protection Act. They are taken in charge, but since the court does not have sufficient means to assure them the proper educative assistance, they keep coming back. They seem to learn to steal as time goes on. The second common denominator, is the progressive seriousness of the offences, as well as the increasing amounts of money they manage to procure. The third common denominator is their poor school record. All these youngsters, with the exception of one (Dossier No. 13), were expelled from schools many times, had poor marks, and received an education for inferior to that of boys of the same age.

It should be noted, furthermore, that the measures for the protection and treatment of juvenile delinquency overlap as far as placement is concerned, even though they are decided chronologically in a successive manner. First, there is protection under article 15 of the provincial legislation, and there is also delinquency, which comes under federal legislation, that is, the criminal code. Much difference it makes in practice! Children in need of the court's protection, as well as the others, are returned to their parents, even when sometimes (see Dossier No. 4) the child is physically maltreated. One can only hope that the provincial legislation on physically maltreated children will correct this amazing state of affairs.

Today as in the past, however, social workers are asked to avoid placing a child outside his natural home if at all possible. Study of the fourteen dossiers gives reason to believe that all these cases result from natural parents who are criminals, sick, indifferent, hostile, or incapable of looking after their children and whose rights, nonetheless, are much better protected than the interests of the minors concerned. There is no better indication of this than Dossier No. 14. Although his natural mother abandoned him, on many occasions being in prison for infractions she committed, we were satisfied to keep her son confined, in his turn, while waiting to find a home or an institution able to accept him. It was only in 1971, when the boy had already reached the age of seventeen, that "adoption papers were forwarded to the society for adoption," as mentioned in the dossier. However, the mother opposed this, and the boy continued to lead a marginal existence. I would like to consider this an exceptional case, but I cannot but question the entire system of adoption as it exists here, as well as its terms and conditions.

It is obvious that every sociojudicial system has a certain percentage of failures, but its successes, on the other hand, are generally unknown. This is so because there are no records kept of those who appear only once before the Juvenile Court and never return. However, there is nothing to prevent us from claiming, with the aid of theoretical and empirical experience, that those who answer for a single offence before a judge and subsequently reform have family support that is sufficiently strong to help them without society having to intervene. In other words, it is on the files of recidivists, minors whose true parents are unable to or do not want to fulfill their responsibilities, that, in my opinion, research should be done in order to find the basic causes of the marginal behavior of the children concerned, to analyze the stages of their evolution, and to look for the best way of helping them.

However, the dossiers concerning youngsters referred by the Juvenile Court to a court for adults, which should serve to inform the latter's judge, are amazingly incomplete. They do not include resumés of the reports from the institutions or the opinions of the social workers involved in the case, not to mention those of the probation officers charged by the judge to help the child and his family. When reading the particulars, written in the briefest possible terms, concerning why the request was made for the child's protection by the court, it would be useful, I believe, to know who asked for this protection and as a result of what investigations or facts discovered by the police, social workers, or parents themselves.

It seems inconceivable to think of establishing preventive policies as long as we take for granted the total irresponsibility of parents and the no less than total respect for their rights. It is an illusion to believe that by keeping a child in detention because his mother is in prison we are accomplishing prevention. In other words, it is impossible to plan preventive policies unless two elements are available: precise statistical data for each neighborhood and region and comparative analyses based on data concerning the delinquent behavior of adolescents in time and geographical space. A third basic element, moreover, is the designing of a model individual file comprising socioeducational and judicial information about the natural parents, the foster families, if any, and the minors concerned.

In effect, sociojudicial action is, in principle, a means of protecting children and helping the family, but as it exists today, it is often the defender of society against delinquent minors and not a framework capable of fostering prevention. When one reads, as in Dossier No. 7, that the child of a recidivist and a prostitute is systematically sent back home by the court, sometimes at the request of the mother, sometimes of the father, one cannot help but questioning whether a protection officer can really help a young boy under such conditions and give him the assistance necessary to get him used to a way of life that is proper for his development. When we see that such was not the case, since the boy in question becomes a recidivist, we are not surprised. When finally, after stating the reasons the case was transferred to the Court of Sessions of the Peace, we learn that the juvenile judge recommends "a stay of two years at Saint Vincent de Paul to learn a trade," and we know that this is a federal penitentiary, we cannot help but feel that the judge, having no other course of action, has resorted in desperation to black humor.

Notes

1. Gabrielle, Roy, *Bonheur d'occasion* (Montreal: Beauchemin, 1947).
2. Source: *Annuaire du Québec 1975-1976.*
3. Source: *Annuaire du Québec 1975-1976.* Unfortunately, the statistics compiled include all children up to the age of twenty, and not up to the age of eighteen.
4. For details, see Parizeau, *Ces jeunes qui nous font peur* (Montreal: René Ferron, 1974).

3 Juvenile Delinquency and the Family

What do we mean by prevention? The term *prevention* is used in sociology and criminology, as well as in certain legislation, as a euphemism for punishment or repression of crime. Thus in studies on the preventive role of the police, we describe the action taken by a night patrol in marginal neighborhoods as "police prevention," or we speak of the placement of a minor in a reform school as "preventive action." Similarly, when it is considered dangerous to release a hardened criminal on parole prior to his appearance before a judge, we say he is "in preventive detention," and a juvenile delinquent can be sentenced to prison "as a preventive measure."

These few remarks are relevant to the subject examined in this chapter, namely, society's intervention in the lives of criminogenic families. We define the latter in accordance with the results obtained by Sheldon and Eleanor Glueck, whose works in criminology are considered classics.

Prevention Indicators

Over a period of many years, the Gluecks had undertaken a systematic study of 500 delinquents and 500 nondelinquents, taking the genetic aspects into consideration, as well as growth of intelligence, progress at school, and general behavior. On page 278 of their book *Unravelling Juvenile Delinquency*, published in 1950, they give certain definitions that we have adopted as basic. Hence the following citation:

> Character is the result of training as well as of natural equipment. Mechanisms of sublimation and of constructive or harmless energy canalization, as well as "knowledge of right and wrong", are part of the apparatus of character expression, a boy does not express himself in a vacuum but in a cultural milieu ranging from the intimate, emotionladen atmosphere of the home to that of the school, the neighborhood, and general society. Primitive tendencies are morally and legally neutral. . . .

> How did the home conditions of the delinquents and nondelinquents in this study tend to facilitate or hamper the process of internalization of authority, the taming and sublimation of primitive impulses, and the definition of standards of good and bad?

> To answer this significant question requires, first, a review of the findings concerning the background of the parents of the boys; for the

parents are not only the products of the biologic and cultural systems in which they were born and reared, but also the transmitters of that biosocial heritage to their children. We found that while the divergencies between the delinquents and nondelinquents were sometimes not as marked as those found in other aspects of the research, the biosocial legacy of the parents of the delinquents was consistently poorer than that of the nondelinquents. There was a greater incidence of emotional disturbances, mental retardation, alcoholism, and criminalism among the families of the mothers of the delinquents. These differences existed despite the fact that the economic condition of the homes in which the mothers of the delinquent boys had been reared was not very different from that of the homes in which the mothers of the nondelinquents grew up. In the families of the fathers of the delinquents, also, there was more emotional disturbance and criminalism than among the families of the fathers of the nondelinquents.

Thus, to the extent that the parents of the boys communicated the standards and ideals of their own rearing to that of their children, it is evident that the social—and perhaps, partially also, biologic—legacy of the delinquents was worse than that of the nondelinquents.

As for the parents themselves, their biosocial handicaps should be considered as at least partly influencing their capacity to rear their children properly. A higher proportion of the parents of the delinquents suffered from serious physical ailments, were mentally retarded, emotionally disturbed, alcoholic, and—most significant—many more of them had a history of delinquency. . . .

On the basis of the Gluecks' findings, one could have hoped for a reorientation of the exploratory works done on the prevention of juvenile delinquency. Logically, their findings should have given rise to a thorough study of the attitudes of parents and the elaboration of preventive policies aimed at reeducating the parental couple or the family. The fact is that from 1950 until today, research on families has been done only a posteriori, when the child is already in the hands of the sociolegal services, owing to the traditional reticence of communities.

The myth of the sanctity of motherhood is so strongly entrenched, it seems, that it inspires a reluctance to investigate the parents when trying to find out what is responsible for the children's unhappy state. Better to look after victim children and delinquent minors. The fact remains, as we have seen in the preceding pages, that the process of delinquency is a result of the regression and deviance that occurs during the evolution of the child, and that, considering the rapidity of this evolution and its importance in a life cycle, this process often becomes irreversible.

The term *prevention*, then, should include above all the study of the behavior of parents and of assistance to the family that would check the problem behavior of the children. To believe in a society without criminals is utopian, but perhaps it is not beyond the realm of possibility to at least reduce the criminality of children by trying to inform and educate certain categories of families.

In order to study families that are particularly unstable, I have chosen a target group composed of male prisoners of the Montreal Detention Center (Bordeaux Prison), recidivists, and female prisoners at Maison Tanguay (women's prison) who said they had children and were willing to answer my questions.

The first phase of my research consisted of preparing two questionnaires, the first addressed to prisoners, the second to their families. In addition to general questions, some related to the prisoners' aspirations concerning lifestyles, scales of values, tastes, or ambitions, as well as the type of future desired for their children.

The Families of Prisoners and the Transmission of Values

I have tried to evaluate the importance attached to certain values, such as work, religion, or tradition, as well as the women's attitude toward the men in prison and how these attitudes are reflected in the information transmitted to the children. I have tried as well to obtain the maximum information on the children's school situations, their state of health, and their relations with their mother, father, and the rest of the family. Once drafted, the questionnaires were twice revised in the light of comments from the practitioners and people involved in the research.

Attempts to evaluate family attachments through the exchange of letters and gifts on anniversaries and holidays, such as Christmas, proved difficult. This was due to purely technical reasons: among others, the restrictive regulations of the detention centers and the inability of many to write, observable not only among the children, but among the adults as well.

Besides administering the questionnaire, which was filled in by the interviewer of the person or persons concerned, during the interviews with the family, a discussion of 1 or 2 hours took place and was written down in each case. The pages that follow present not only recapitulation tables of the answers obtained, but also additional explanations that were given verbatim by the prisoners and their families.

The choice of the sample was based on criteria derived from the criminal records of the inmates. I decided to use only the dossiers of people who had served several terms in prison, who had had a number of previous sentences, or who had been sentenced for serious crimes. I wanted to study the family situation of prisoners who had managed to maintain ties with their family, but were frequently away from their children or absent for relatively prolonged periods. Many criminologists, sociologists, and psychologists uphold the theory that the maintaining of family ties and a sense of responsibility toward children is a powerful agent in the social reintegration of delinquents. On the basis of this hypothesis, I took for granted that such people would be more apt than their peers to be concerned about the welfare and development of their children. It must be said, however, that contrary to this theory, since these prisoners are not first offenders, their attachment to their families does not seem to be sufficient reason to deter them from recidivating. Thus theories are not always proven correct in every case.

I do not intend to discuss this phenomenon here for the very good reason that I am not interested in the adults per se, but in their children and in the values they transmit to them. Since the results I have obtained are considerably different for men than for women prisoners, I shall present and comment on them separately.

Prisoners and Their Families

Between October 31 and December 29, 1977, when I selected the dossiers for my investigation, there were 679 prisoners at the Montreal Detention Center, distributed among the five wings of the prison. Sections A and B house prisoners serving short sentences, section C is reserved for recidivists having already served time in prisons or penitentiaries, section D is the receiving center, and section E is mainly for first offenders.

On arrival, all prisoners fill out an admission form, and of those who were in prison for the second time or had already served several previous terms, thirty-one stated that they had more than one dependent. Since I wanted to analyze the situation of men who had children and who officially recognized them, I chose these thirty-one dossiers. There was no point in trying to track down the children of fathers who no longer lived with them. My objective was not to look for the probability of genetic consequences, but to discern how a delinquent family evaluates the needs of children and what values it transmits to a growing child.

Of the thirty-one dossiers, five could not be studied because three of the prisoners were released a short time after I began my study and two others preferred not to answer the questionnaire or be interviewed. Thus I analyzed twenty-six dossiers selected from 700 that were in the files at the time and that the director of the prison kindly placed at my disposal. Of the twenty-six dossiers, twenty-three concerned prisoners in section C, which at this time housed 166 inmates, and represented 14 percent of this group. The other three were lodged in another wing, but also had had previous prison records and were therefore recidivists.

For each dossier, I first took down the personal information as stated by the prisoner on entering the prison and then the details concerning his criminal record, the sentence served, previous sentences, the type of infraction, and the nature of the penalty, including fines, parole, and detention. During the interviews and the filling out of the questionnaire, I asked further questions regarding personal data, such as age, marital status, and last employment prior to the sentence, as well as facts about the prisoner's parents, their profession, and the relationship maintained with them.

The answers obtained corresponded with those shown on the administration forms, although these are not officially verified, and it is possible that the prisoners occasionally give information that is imagined or false. It seems, however, that inmates generally do not try to change or improve the facts about themselves. This confirmed the possibility of compiling valid statistics concerning the profile of the prisoners, even though the basic information had never been submitted to controls as such.

The twenty-six prisoners concerned were informed of the objectives of my research and agreed to see me and give me the addresses of their wives so that I and my assistants could visit them at home and talk to them.

The director of the detention center placed a private room at my disposal, some distance away from those regularly used. It is a room about 100 feet square furnished with a large table and some chairs. The evening before the interview I telephoned the secretary of the prison and gave him the list of prisoners I was to see the next day in order for preparations to be made for the visits. The interviewer then came to the visiting room alone and a guard brought the inmate. The interviews lasted from 30 minutes to 1½ hours. During this time the interviewer filled out the questionnaire and then had a discussion with the prisoner, writing a verbatim report of the conversation. On another occasion, the same interviewer contacted the prisoner's family and went to the wife's home, where he spent an average of 2 hours. See tables 3-1 through 3-5.

Explanation of the Abbreviations in Tables 3-1 through 3-5

Marital status of prisoner		of parents	
M	Married	Y	Yes
S	Separated	N	No

C   Common law wife   D   Dossier of prisoner
D   Divorced

Preference of residence: city/country

CIT   City
C   Country

Prison activities according to availability

A   Television, radio
B   Sports
C   Manual work
D   Reading
E   Prisoners' Committee
F   Others

Prisoners trade

ST   Same trade as his father

Livelihood of the family

SW   Social welfare

Contacts with the family

M   Mother
F   Father
W   Wife
C   Common-law wife
Ch   Children
O   Others
1F   First family
2F   Second family
Q.n.a. Questions not answered

Explanatory remarks concerning the children

3   The children of his first family do not know.
13   Idem.
13   Idem.
24   He is not longer in contact with his first family since 1968 and there-
      fore doesn't know if they know.

Table 3-1
Compilation of the Questionnaire Administered to Prisoners: Profile of the Prisoners

No.	Age	Marital Status	Schooling	Profession	What Profession Would You Have Liked?	Regular Work before Prison	Type of Work	Residence: City or Country	Move from One Area to Another	Activities in Prison
1	35	M	7	Bricklayer (D)	—	Y	—	—	—	—
2	—	S	—	—	—	N	—	—	—	E
3	33	C	11	Painter (D)	—	Y	—	C	N	—
4	29	M	9	Bricklayer	—	N	—	C	N	A B C
5	40	S	7	Mechanic	—	Y	Mechanic	—	Y	A B C D E
6	39	C	17	Bookkeeper	—	Y	Bookkeeper	C	N	A C
7	31	D	9	Chauffeur (7)	Fireman	Y	Mechanic; Knitting factory	C	N	A C
8	43	M	3	Upholsterer	—	Y	Upholstering	C	N	A C
9	38	C	11	Constr. (9)	Prison Admin.	—	—	—	—	—
10	29	M	10	Constr.	—	N	—	Cit.	Y	D
11	32	C	10	Mechanic (11)	Mechanic	Y	Mechanic	C	Y	A B C D F
12	30	M	10	Constr. (12)	Electronics	N	—	C	N	D
13	30	D	9	Chauffeur	Chauffeur	Y	Chauffeur	C	N	C D
14	29	M	8	Mechanic	Mechanic	Part time	Mechanic	C	N	A B C D E F
15	43	M	7	Businessman	Businessman	Y	Businessman	C	N	A D
16	26	C	12	Mechan./for. (16)	Foreman	Y	Operator	C	Y	A C D
17	28	M	10	Chauffeur	Chauffeur	Y	Chauffeur	C/Cit.	N	A B
18	25	C	11	Constr. (18)	Music	Part time	Truck	C	Y	A D F
19	45	M	7	Hotelkeeper	Hotelkeeper	Y	Hotelkeeper	C	Y	B C D
20	38	M	10	No trade (20)	Real estate agent	N	Trucking Co.	C	—	A C E
21	29	M	8	Chauffeur	Chauffeur	Part time	—	C	N	D F
22	36	M	7	Barman	Barman	Y	Barman	Cit.	N	A D
23	37	M	9	Singer	Singer	Y	Singer	Cit.	Y	A B D
24	31	S	12	Painter/cook	Mechanic	Y	Chauffeur	C	Y	B C
25	31	M	4	Lumberman	Lumberman	N	—	C	Y	A D
26	43	M	12	Parts dealer	"Gambling"	Y	Parts dealer	C	Y	B D
Total 34 (agerage)		15 M, 6 C, 3 S, 2 D	9.2 (average)			16 Yes, 7 No, 3 Part time		4 Q.n.a., 18 C, 3 Cit., 1 C/Cit.	12 No, 10 Yes, 4 Q.n.a.	15A, 10B, 11C, 15D, 4E, 5F

Table 3-2
Compilation of the Questionnaire Administered to Prisoners: "Prior to Your Union, Did you Live With. . .?"

No.	Your Parents?	Until What Age?	Your Mother?	Was She Working?	Is She Dead?	Your Father?	Was He Working?	Type of Work	Is He Dead?
1	—	—	—	—	N(D)	—	—	—	Y
2	—	—	—	—	Y	—	—	—	Y
3	—	—	—	—	Y(3)	—	—	—	Y
4	Y	—	Y	N	N	Y	Y	Chauffeur	Y
5	N	—	N	N	Y	N	N	—	Y
6	Y	21	Y	N	N	Y	Y	Foreman	N
7	Y	7	Y	N	Y	Y	Y	Reception of goods	N
8	Y	—	Y	Y	Y	Y	Y	City of Montreal	Y(8)
9	Y	12	Y	—	N(D)	Y	Y	(does not remember)	Y
10	Y	—	Y	N	N(D)	Y	Y	Construction	N(D)
11	Y	14	Y	N	N	Y	Y	Farmer	N
12	Y	25	Y	Y	N	Y	Y	Repairman	N
13	N	16	N	N	N	N	N	—	Disappeared
14	Y	—	Y	Y	N	N	N	—	N
15	Y	20	Y	N	N	Y	Y	Wrought iron worker	N
16	Y	14	Y	N	N	Y	Y	Steward (trains)	N
17	Y	15	Y	N	N	Y	Y	Construction	N
18	Y	16	Y	N	N	Y	Y	Bricklayer	Disappeared (18)
19	Y	18	Y	N	Y	Y	Y	Day laborer	N
20	Y	17	Y	N	N	Y	Y	Painter	Y
21	Y	17	Y	N	Y	Y	Y	Janitor	N
22	Y	21	Y	Y	N	Y	Y	Foreman	N
23	Y	17	Y	N	N	Y	Y	City of Montreal	N
24	Y	16	Y	Y	N	Y	Y	Painter (m.m.)	N
25	Y	18	Y	N	N	N	N	—	N
26	Y	18	Y	N	N	Y	Y	Salesman (m.m.)	N
Total	5 Q.n.a. 21 Yes 2 No	6 Q.n.a. 16.2 (average)	3 Q.n.a. 21 Yes 2 No	4 Q.n.a. 17 No 5 Yes	19 No 7 Yes	3 Q.n.a. 19 Yes 4 No	3 Q.n.a. 19 Yes 4 No	3 Q.n.a.	16 No 8 Yes 2 Disappeared

Table 3-3
Compilation of the Questionnaire Administered to Prisoners: "Recently Were You Living With. . .?"

No.	Your Wife	Age	Was She Working?	Type of Work?	Your Children?	Do They Know You Are in Prison?	Your Common-Law Wife?	Is She Working?	Your Common-Law Wife and Her Children?	Person to Advise in Case of Emergency
1	Y	—	N	—	Y	-	—	—	—	—
2	N(sep)	—	N	—	N	No contact since 1970	—	—	—	—
3	—	—	—	—	—	-	—	—	Y	Mother
4	Y	29	N	—	Y	Y(3)	Y	—	—	Wife
5	N(sep)	—	N	—	Y	N	Y(28 years)	N	Y and N	Common-law wife
6	—	—	Y	Cook	—	Two out of three	Y(24 years)	Y(secretary)	Y	Father
7	N(sep)	—	Y	Nurse	N	They are placed.	Y(24 years)	Y	—	Mother-in-law
8	Y	—	Y	—	Y	Y	—	—	—	Son and wife
9	—	—	—	—	—	N	Y	—	Y	Common-law wife
10	Y	31	N	—	Y	N	—	N	Y	Wife
11	—	—	—	—	Y	-	Y	N	N	Common-law wife
12	Y	23	—	—	Y	N	—	—	Y	Wife
13	N(div)	30	N	—	N	- (13)	Y(24 years)	N	Y	Wife
14	Y	28	N	—	Y	Y	—	—	—	Wife
15	Y	—	Y	At their restaurant	Y	Y	—	—	—	Wife
16	—	—	—	—	Y	Age 14 months	Y(19 years)	N	N	Common-law wife
17	Y	38	N	—	Y	Y	—	—	—	Common-law wife
18	—	—	—	—	N	No contact for 9 years	—	—	—	Mother
19	Y	—	Y	At their hotel	Y	Y	—	—	—	Wife
20	Y	38	N	—	Y	Y	—	—	—	Wife
21	Y	33	N	—	Y	N	—	—	—	Mother
22	Y	38	N	—	Y	-	—	—	—	Wife
23	Y	29	N	—	Y	Y	—	—	—	Wife
24	N(sep)	—	—	—	N	- (24)	Y	N	Y	Common-law wife
25	Y	27	N	—	Y	N	—	—	—	Wife
26	Y	—	Y	Office	Y	Y	—	—	—	Sister-in-law
Total	15 Yes / 5 No / 6 Not married		14 No / 5 Yes / 1 Q.n.a.	18 Yes / 5 No / 3 No children of their own but look after their wife's children		9 Yes / 7 No / 5 Q.n.a.	8 Yes / 3 Live alone / 15 With wife	1 Q.n.a. / 6 No / 1 Yes	5 Yes / 2 No / 1 Yes and No	1 Father; 3 mothers; 1 mother-in-law; 1 sister-in-law; 12 wives; 6 common-law wives; 2 q.n.a.

Table 3-4
Compilation of the Questionnaire Administered to Prisoners: Prisoners' Children

No.	No. of Dependents	Number of Children	Age	Who Do They Live With?	Who Looks After Their Upkeep?
1	6	5	14, 12, 11, 9, 1	Mother	SW
2	6	6	20, 19, 15, 12, 11, 9	?	He does not know
3	4	3	12, 10, 5	Mother	SW
4	4	3	7, 4, 3	Two with mother one placed	SW
5	3	3	19, 17, 7	Two with common-law wife	SW
6	2	2	8, 6	Placed	SW
7	2	2	10, 7	Mother	Mother
8	4	3	19, 15, 10	Mother	Mother
9	2	1	12	Mother	SW
10	4	3	8, 4, 2	Mother	SW
11	2	2	4, 1	Mother	SW
12	3	2	2, 4	Mother	SW
13	4	1	4	Mother	SW
14	3	3	7, 5, 2	Mother	SW
15	5	4	20, 19, 17, 15	two with mother two hospital	Have a restaurant
16	2	1	1	Mother	SW
17	3	2	13, 7	Mother	SW
18	2	1	9	Mother	Mother
19	4	3	23, 22, 18	Mother	Have an hotel
20	6	5	18, 16, 14, 13, 11	Mother	SW
21	2	2	6, 3	Mother	SW
22	2	1	15	Mother	Refused to say
23	5	5	11, 9, 5, 4, 3	Mother	SW
24	4	3	14, 12, 8	Mother	SW
25	3	3	8, 5, 2	Mother	SW
26	0	3	23, 22, 18	Mother	—
Averages:	3.3	2.8	72 children age: 10.4		1 Q.n.a.
					18 SW
					3 Mothers
					2 Have businesses
					1 Does not know
					1 Refused to say

Table 3-5
Compilation of the Questionnaire Administered to Prisoners: Contacts with the Family or Families (1st and 2nd)

No.	Contacts Maintained	Letters	Who Writes to You?	Visits	Who Visits You?
1	Y	Y	W, Ch	Y	W
2	N	N	–	N	–
3	1F:Y, 2F:Y	1F:N, 2F:Y	2F:C	1F:Y, 2F:Y	1F:Ch, 2F:C
4	Y	Y	W	Y	C
5	1F:Y, 2F:Y	1F:N, 2F:N	F, M, C	1F:Y, 2F:Y	1F:Ch, 2F:Ch
6	Y	Y	–	Y	C
7	Y	N	–	N	–
8	Y	N	–	Y	W, Ch, others
9	Y	N	–	Y	C
10	Y	Y	W, Ch	Y	W
11	Y	Y	C, Ch	Y	C, Ch
12	Y	N	–	Y	W
13	1F:Y, 2F:Y	1F:N, 2F:Y	2F:C	1F:N, 2F:Y	2F:C, Ch
14	Y	Y	W, Ch	Y	W, Ch, others
15	Y	Y	M, W, Ch, others	Y	M, W, Ch
16	Y	Y	W	Y	W, Ch, others
17	Y	Y	W, Ch	Y	W, others, friends
18	Y	Y	M, C, friends	Y (once)	C
19	Y	Y	W, Ch, friends	Y	Ch
20	Y	Y	W, Ch	Y	W
21	Y	N	–	Y	W, others
22	Y	N	–	Y	W, others
23	Y	Y	F, W, Ch	Y	W, Ch
24	1F:N, 2F:Y	1F:N, 2F:Y	2F:C, Ch	1F:N, 2F:Y	2F:F, C, Ch
25	Y	Y	W	N	A friend
26	Y	Y	W, Ch	Y	Ch
Total	25 Yes 1 No	18 Yes 8 No	12W, 11Ch, 6C, 3M, 2F, 2 friends 6 others	23 Yes 3 No	12W, 12CH, 7C, 2 friends, 1F, 1M, 6 others

Disparities between the Dossier and Prisoners' Statements

Marital status and profession

1   States in the dossier that he is married. His common-law wife told us he was not married.
7   Mechanic in the dossier.
9   Day laborer in the dossier
11 Day laborer in the dossier
12 Day laborer in the dossier
13 Married in the dossier
16 Cook's assistant
17 States he lives with common-law wife in the dossier. Corroborated by her.
18 Day laborer in the dossier.
20 Mechanic

Employment

7   States no in the dossier.
11 Idem.
13 Idem.
21 States yes in the dossier.
22 States no in the dossier.

Parents

3   States no in the dossier.
8   States no in the dossier.
18 States yes in the dossier.

To make generalizations on the basis of our sample would be dangerous. However, the data shown in the tables are all the more significant in that they confirm those obtained in various other studies on the prison population. For example, the average age and level of education of the prisoners correspond with those obtained by the administrative authorities for recidivists in general.[1] The same applies to the trades in which the prisoners stated they were engaged, construction and services predominating.

On the subject of trades, some further remarks are in order. First of all, the prisoners' fathers did the same type of work as they did and in all probability experienced the same job insecurity as they, if not greater, given the development of the trade unions in recent years.

I found two foremen among nineteen of the fathers who the prisoners believed were working—a fact that could be considered a sign that they had been promoted. It should be noted, however, that of the total of twenty-six cases, three had nothing to say about their fathers' work, and four stated that theirs had no work. In other words, seven out of twenty-six, or almost one-quarter, grew up in a home where the man of the house had no regular job.

Regarding the prisoners' mothers, numbers five and fourteen did not work. Concerning the parent/child relationships they experienced in their childhood, five prisoners did not live with their parents, two ceased to live with them before the age of ten, and twelve ceased to live with them at the age of eighteen or younger. Thus, of the total of twenty-six prisoners, in the case of five we may presume that there was practically no parental influence, for two it was fairly limited because they were so young, and for the other twelve it was variable since they no longer lived with their parents from the age of twelve in some cases and from the ages of fourteen, fifteen, sixteen, seventeen, or eighteen in others.

During the interviews, some of the prisoners spoke of their childhood in terms that I reproduce here unchanged, indicating the prisoners concerned by number. These numbers correspond with those shown in the list of answers obtained on the questionnaire.

The Prisoners' Comments regarding their Childhood

Prisoner No. 4: "I lived in a poor neighborhood. We were ten children. My father worked as a chauffeur. I started to steal at the age of twelve; so did my two kid brothers, one of whom is now in the next cell. My first term in prison for compound robbery dates back to when I was eighteen. I was sentenced to 2 years in the penitentiary.... I don't want my mother to visit me in prison as she's had enough as it is."

Prisoner No. 5: "I never knew my parents; my mother died in childbirth when I was 2 years old. When I was sixteen, I learned that my father was at Saint-Jean-de-Dieu for the past fourteen years. At a year and a half I was placed in an old people's home, at thirteen I left to work on a farm. . . ."

Prisoner No. 6: "My parents come from the country; my two grandfathers were mayors. My father was a foreman and contractor in housing construction. My parents are living and consider me the black sheep of the family."

Prisoner No. 7: "My parents were born in the country, but came to live in the city. My mother died in childbirth. I was then seven years old. I have a sister. My father used to tell me that I was a mistake [illegitimate child] and didn't look after me. He was working, but I was placed in an orphanage at the age of seven. First with the Grey nuns, the most vicious of all, and at the age of ten with homosexual priests who used to beat me because I did not want to go to the priest's room at night to get candy. I ran away three times and the police brought me back, and at fourteen I began to work in a knitting factory and to steal for kicks. My father was an alcoholic, and me, I'm an alcoholic and a drug addict. I've done everything. I've even stolen from my father. I don't want to see him because it's on account of him that I'm in prison. Only my maternal grandfather ever helped me. He died at the age of a hundred and one."

Prisoner No. 8: Native of Pointe-Saint-Charles; no contact with parents, mother dead, father living.

Prisoner No. 9: "My father died when I was five. He used to work. My mother was left with five children. She was a cleaning woman. We were very poor; we often used to eat moistened bread sprinkled with sugar. All my brothers are working now and I am the only one who has been in prison. I began to steal at the age of twelve and was put in a reform school. I wanted to have something of my own—a car. One of my brothers only had a bicycle at the time...."

Prisoner No. 11: Lived with his parents until the age of fourteen. His father was a manager.

Prisoner No. 13: "My parents were city people and moved to the country. My father was a war veteran; he was in the first commandos; he was a killer and was heartless. When he drank he went crazy and used to beat all the children and even my mother. He left home when I was thirteen and never came back. We were eleven children and were extremely poor. One of my brothers is in prison, like me, but not the others, who are working and have good jobs. I was placed at the age of seven. It was to protect me from my father. I entered Mont Saint-Antoine when I was eleven and escaped from there twenty-six times. I used to go home to my mother. At fifteen, I started to steal and drink. I didn't like to steal, but I went along with my friends. I like to fight. I got married when I was seventeen because I couldn't get along with my mother who often threw me out...."

Prisoner No. 14: "We were eight children, all placed. It was better. My father was in prison and used to drink. I have a brother in the penitentiary. I was at Saint-Vallier.[2] I began to work in construction at fourteen. All the men there used to drink and me, I learned too. I never steal sober; I'm too scared."

Prisoner No. 17: "We were five children. I was the 'no good' of the family and I was beaten by my father and by my mother at every school report. My friends at the time were all criminals. I left the house at fifteen to work in construction. Afterwards I worked in a butcher shop; I got married at twenty; I had my first contact with the law at that age following assault and battery on a policeman during a hockey game."

Prisoner No. 18: "I began to steal at the age of five for 'kicks.' I used to steal French books from school, but couldn't read French [Anglophone]. At sixteen, I went to Toronto to get mescaline and made more money than the police. My mother was good, but my father treated me like an illegitimate child. He used to drink a lot. My parents have been separated for ten years. We were four children."

Prisoner No. 19: "We were seven children. I am the only one to have been in prison. I worked as a guitarist in night clubs. I committed my first offence at twenty-eight."

Prisoner No. 20: "We were eight children. My father was a mild man, my mother very strict. She wanted to do too much, in the old style, too severe. The family was not in need. I began to steal around the age of four or five, in the stores. At six or seven I made the rounds of the telephone booths. I would block the money return mechanism. I used to steal and I still steal today, mainly for the 'trip.' I was always in trouble with the police. I met real thieves at the juvenile court. I had an auto at fourteen. I joined the navy at seventeen to be able to travel. One of my brothers was sentenced to twenty-seven years in penitentiary...."

Prisoner No. 21: "We were four children, all placed on farms or in institutions. I was placed from the age of seven till I was ten, then at Huberdeau,[3] where I was for two years. At fourteen, I used to steal autos with others for 'kicks.' I spent a year at Mont St. Antoine.[4] Sober, I am not a thief and have never been able to steal."

Prisoner No. 23: "We were four at home. My father spent twenty-two years in prison. My mother could never manage, either with the children or with her budget. We lived in poverty. At the age of eight, I was head of a gang in 'Faubourg à la mélasse.'[5] We all became very difficult when we learned that papa was in prison. One of my brothers was sentenced to five years in penitentiary at the age of eighteen."

Prisoner No. 24: "We were two adopted children. My mother was ill and my father used to drink, beat her, and beat us. I have two scars on my face because my father threw me against a chair. I fought with my father once when he beat up my mother. I beat the tar out of him and he chased me down the street with a rifle, but now we get along well. My parents were divorced when I was eight years old. My mother drinks and lives with another man. I did my first shoplifting at fourteen. I began to work at sixteen and married a woman of twenty-three, on an impulse, at seventeen. My brother has never been in prison and doesn't want to see me."

Prisoner No. 25: "My mother died when I was two. We were four. My father remarried a widow who also had four children. We were eight and extremely poor. My father didn't drink, but spent everything on women. They were separated when I was eight. I was placed by the Juvenile Court even though I wasn't bad and was going to school. I was in five or six foster homes till I was fourteen. I didn't like it. My second mother left again with her four children. She was a good mother, but all the same, alone, she couldn't look after her four children and the four of the husband she had divorced. My first thefts were not because of need but to have something of my own. My brother did seven years in penitentiary, but not my sisters. In the three times, I did nine years in penitentiary."

Prisoner No. 26: "I had a very happy childhood. My family was very close and still is."

What is evident from these confessions is that these people come from diverse milieus, but ones that are generally poor, dissolute, or criminogenic. Among the common denominators, I am concerned with three constants.

First of all, the prisoners admit that they started to steal when very young and that no punishment could stop them. Many theories about punishment's lack of dissuasive effect could be based on this fact, but this is not my purpose. What I believe is essential to point out is that the prisoners were unable to develop properly during their childhood, that they did not receive or were unable to assimilate the models of behavior in society suggested to them by the services responsible or their parents, as was the case for prisoners number 6 and 26, for example, and that they continue to lead marginal existences as adults.

The question, then, is: What values do these prisoners transmit to their children, who number a total of seventy-two for the entire group? Some are their own children and some are those of their common-law wives, but they look after them and fulfill the role of father when they are not in prison. To answer this question, I interviewed the prisoners' wives and living companions who look after the children in their absence.

Families of the Prisoners

Of the twenty-six prisoners I met at the Montreal Detention Center, two told me that they had lost contact with their family, one said that his wife was living outside of Montreal, and six refused authorization for a visit to their living companions or wives. Of the seventeen families I was able to contact, one had just moved and had a privately listed telephone number, while in two other cases, I met with the mother and mother-in-law of the prisoner, respectively, not the wife. Thus I obtained answers to the questionnaire and interviews with fifteen of the prisoners' wives or living companions, one mother, and one mother-in-law, and they were all seen at home.

The numbers in the recapitulation tables (tables 3-6 through 3-10) indicate the prisoners concerned and replace their names, but they do not signify numerical order; consequently, they are not in sequence.

By means of the questionnaire, I tried first of all to gather all the personal data concerning the prisoner's common-law wife, then the facts of the work situation before and after the union, and then I tried to assess the woman's attitude toward the man and his conduct and her ideas about bringing up children and the transmitting of certain traditions.

Finally, I asked questions about the financial situation, and it was here that the answers were easiest to interpret and most surprising. As will be seen in tables 3-6 through 3-10, fourteen women out of fifteen live on welfare without having the assistance of a social worker. The one exception is number 24, whose situation, according to the interview with the prisoner, is the following:

I want to get a divorce in order to marry my common-law wife. She is a good woman. She is ill and is forty, whereas I am only thirty-one. She is very poor. The fridge is often empty. She has only an electric heater for a six-room apartment. Her children are a problem. The eldest, age 12, is mentally and physically retarded. He suffered a shock when he lost his father at the age of seven. He set fire to the block where he lived. A whole wall burnt down. The best thing would be to place him in a special school during the week. He goes to the same school as his brother, who is eight years old and in second grade. It's not a special school. The daughter started to steal at fourteen, but she doesn't like it. Youth Assistance sent her back to school; she didn't want to go any more. She went to spend a week with her real father. Her mother and I didn't like that . . . "after all he did to your mother. . . ." She has sex with boys who come right up to the house and whistle at her mother, because from the back, they look alike.

In short, the intervention of a social worker in this one and only case was because of the delinquency of the children, who were known to the police, and the illness of the mother (according to the prisoner, she suffers from nervous depression), but not necessarily because of a concern for prevention, in the strict sense of the term.

On the basis of the answers to the questionnaire given by the prisoners' common-law wives, the following general comments can be made. Their average age is slightly under that of the men, and we find very young girls, like number 16, who was only sixteen when she moved in with the prisoner. The length of time certain couples stayed together seems to show that a greater attachment developed when the ties were established when they were very young, as was the case for number 20, where both were only eighteen. The same applies to couples 1 and 10.

Based on the types of trades their fathers' practiced, the family backgrounds of the two partners are fairly comparable, with a slightly higher level of income in the cases of the women.

Table 3-6
Interviews with the Families of Prisoners: Past Record

No.	Age	Birthplace	Brothers	Sisters	Total	Duration of Marriage or Union in Years	Schooling	Specialization	Father	Mother
1	32	C	—	—	—	15	6	None	Raised animals	—
3	32	C	—	—	—	2	2	Barmaid	—	Did not work
4	29	Cit.	0	0	1	6	9	None	—	Did not work
7	32	Cit. (town)	1	2	4	3	11	Commercial	Working	Did not work
9	35	C	—	—	—	9	10	None	—	—
10	33	Cit. (town)	4	3	8	11	11	Commercial	Foreman	Charwoman
12	24	C	3	4	8	2 (?)	3	None	City empl.	Did not work
13	24	Cit. (town)	0	2	3	2	11	None	Foreman	Did not work
16	19	C	0	1	2	3	11	Secretary	Proprietor camping and mechanic	Owner of lingerie shop
17	38	Cit. (town)	4	1	6	8	10	Secretary	—	—
20	38	Cit.	4	2	7	20	9	Asst. book-keeper	Carpenter	Did not work
21	35	Cit.	2	1	4	8	9	Secretary	Railroad	Did not work
23	29	C	2	2	5	9	8	None	City empl.	Did not work
24	40	Cit.	0	1	2	5	2	None	Doesn't know; killed in the war	Did not work
25	27	Cit. (town)	3	1	5	7	7	None	Lumberman	Teacher
Total: 15	31.1	6C 4Cit. 5Cit. (towns)	1.9	1.7	4.6	7.3	8.1	1 Barmaid 1 Asst. book-keeper 2 Businessmen 3 Secretaries	4 Q.n.a. 10 Worked 1 Didn't know	3 Q.n.a. 6 Worked 6 Did not work

Note: Cit. = city; C = country.

Table 3-7
Interviews with the Families of Prisoners: Work

No.	Did You Work Before Your Marriage? Yes — Part Time	Full Time	Type of Work	No	Have You Worked since the Birth of Your Children? Yes — Part Time	Full Time	Type of Work	No	Are You Working Now? No	Yes	Nq
1		X	Factory			X	Waitress		X		
3	X		Factory			X	Waitress (3 wks)				X
4		X	Waitress			X	Cook			Full-time cook	
7				X	Nights						X
9		X	Manager of store			X	Proprietor of cleaning est.				X
10		X	Factory		Nights (12 wks)						X
12	X		Private home					X	X		
13				X				X	X		
16				X				X	X		
17		X	Secretary (hospital)		Nights		In a hospital				X
20		X	Office and factory								X
21		X				X	Factory				X
23	X		Waitress						X		
24		X	Private home						X		
25		X	Cashier						X		
Total: 15	3	9		3	3	5		3	7	1	7

Table 3-8
Interviews with the Families of Prisoners: Attitudes

No.	Was Your Husband Arrested at Home? Yes	No	In Your Opinion, Is Your Husband A Victim of Society?	A Strong Man?	A Weak Man?	Do Your Children Know Their Father Is in Prison? Yes[a]	No[a]
1				X		X	
3					X	X	
4					X		X
7	X		X		X		X
9				X			X
10		X			X		X
12		X		X			X
13		X			X	X	
16	X			X		Too young	
17		X	X	X		X	
20	X				X	X	
21		X	X	X	X		X
23		X	X			X	
24	X		X			X	
25		X			X	X	
Total: 15	4 Yes 7 No 4 Q.n.a.		1 A victim and a weak man 1 A victim and a strong man 1 A bit of all three			8 Yes 6 No 1 Too young	

Table 3-8 continued

No.			Do You Visit Your Husband Every Week?				
	Yes	No	Alone	With the Children	By Bus	By Car	With Someone
1	X		X				
3	X			X		X	
4	X			X	X		
5		X (7)					
9	X		X			X	
10	X (sometimes every 2 wks)			X	X		
12	X (every 2 wks because its far)		X				Father-in-law
13	X		X		X		
16	X			X	X		
17	X		X		X		
20	X		X	X (twice)	X		
21	X		X				A relative
23	X			X	X	Car being repaired	
24	X		X	X (once)			
25		X (25)					
Total: 15	11 Yes 1 Sometimes every 2 wks 1 Every 2 wks 2 No	8 7 (7): (25):	8 Alone 7 And/or with the children Hasn't seen him for a year Prisoner does not want her to visit him		8 By bus 2 By car 2 With someone else 1 Q.n.a.		

Table 3-8 continued

No.	Do You Attend Church on Sunday		Do You Attend Midnight Mass Every Year?			
	Yes	No	Yes	No	Alone	With the Children
1		X (1)		X (1)		They go alone
3		X	X			X
4		X		X		
7		X		X		
9		X	X			Sometimes
10		X		X		
12		X		X		
13		X		X		
16		X		X		
17		X		X		
20		X (20)		X		
21		X	X (21)		X	
23		X (23)	X (23)			
24		X		X		X
25		X		X		
Total 15:		15 No	4 Yes 11 No			1 Alone 1 The children go alone 2 With the children

(1): Doesn't go because she has to look after the baby
(20): Only once a year
(21): Not this year
(23): Not this year

aIn these two columns, X represents a family and not a child.

Table 3-9
Interviews with the Families of Prisoners: Children

No	Do Your Children Live with You?		Were They Ever Placed Elsewhere?						Do Your Children Go to School?	
	Yes	No	Yes					No	Yes	No
			By Whom?	Where?	At What Age?	For How Long?	For What Reason?			
1	X		(1) Mother	Mother's sister	10, 9, 4	1 year	Mother was working	X(1)	X	
3	X								X	
4	2 out of 3 (4)		Court	Receiving center	7	Indefinite	Protection		X	
7		X	Mother	Mother's parents	10, 7	Indefinite	Mother works		X	
9	X							X	X	
10	X							X	X	
12	X							X	X	
13	X							X	X	
16	X							X		X
17	X		Mother	Mother's brother	5	2 years	Q.n.a.			X
20	X							X	X	
21	X							X	X	
23	X							X	X	
24	X		Social Welfare	Foster homes	9, 6, 3	1½ years			X	
25	X						Mother in hospital	X	X	

Total 15:
13 Yes
1 No
1 2 out of 3

5 families: Children have or had been placed
10 families: Children never placed

13 Yes
2 No, too young

(1): The prisoner told us that the children had already been placed by social welfare, and it had been difficult to get them back. His told us they had never been placed.

(4): The wife is waiting for a foster home for the other two.

Table 3-9 continued

No.	Do Their Friends Know Where Their Father Is?		Do The Principal and Teachers Know?		What Type of Students Are Your Children?				Total of Marks Obtained Last Year	Are Your Children Regularly Examined By a Doctor?	
	Yes	No	Yes	No	Poor	Average	Gifted	Very gifted		Yes	No
1		X		X	X	X	X		1 got 70%; the others ?	X	Never
3	X			X		X			She doesn't remember	X	
4		X	X			X			He had to repeat	X	
7		X		X		X			Q.n.a.		Not often
9		X		X			X		Almost 75% (not sure)	X	
10		X		X		X			Above average since he repeated	X	
12		X		X			X		Did not go	X	
13										X	
16										X	
17		X		X		X			76%	X	
20	X(20)			X		X		X	Q.n.a.	X	
21	X(21)			X	X				Poor	X	
23	X		X				X		Q.n.a.	X	
24		X		X		X	X		1: 73, 76, 80% 2: 70, 72%	X	When sick
25		X		X		X	X		Q.n.a.	X	
Total: 15	4 Yes 9 No	2 Yes 11 No			2	9	6	1		12 Yes 3 No	

(20) and (21): Only some of their friends know their father is in prison.

Table 3-9 continued

No.	Have Your Children Ever Been Seriously Ill?		Have Your Children Ever Been in Contact with			If You Had the Choice, What Would You Like Your Children to Become?[a]
	Yes	No	Police?	A Judge?	Social Worker?	
1	X					Seamstress, teacher, and then marriage
3		X				Lawyer, pilot, nurse; no early marriage
4	X				X	Football player and air hostess
7	X					Policeman, pilot, fancy skater
9		X				Lawyer or doctor
10	X		X			Office worker, nurse
12		X	X		X	Waitress; attend school until age 16
13	X		X			Lawyer
16		X		Too young		No choice
17		X	X	X		Lawyer or doctor
20		X	X			No choice
21		X			X	Lawyer or doctor
23	X				X	Lawyer or doctor; the girl is too delicate
24	X		X		X	Plumber, chauffeur; the girl does not need an education
25	X					Chauffeur; the girl does not need a profession

[a]The first answer is nearly always: "Whatever they would like; I leave them free to choose." The second answer (to the same question) is partly the choice of the mother and partly that of the child. In general, the mothers never thought of this question before.
Note: X represents a family and not a child.

Table 3-10
Interviews with the Families of Prisoners: Financial Situation

No.	No. of Moves Since Your Marriage	Enough money? Yes	Enough money? No	His Pay? Yes	His Pay? No	Gifts? Yes	Gifts? No	Heavy Drinker? Yes	Heavy Drinker? No	Gamble? Yes	Gamble? No	Trouble Present?	Trouble Absent?	SW Aid For Yourself	SW Aid For Children	Telephoned Social Services?	Seen a Social Worker?
1	–	X		X(part)		X		X		X			X	X	X	Never	Once
3			X		X(3)	X			X	X			X	X	X	Never	Once/yr
4	21 in 10 yrs.	X(4)			X	X		X					X	X	X	Twice	1 week for last 8 months
7	4		X(7)		X		X					X		X	X		Once/yr
9		X		X		X		X		X			X	X	X	Never	Once/yr
10	4	X(10)			X		X	X				X		X	X	Never	Once/yr
12	4	X		X		X			X				X	X	X	Never	2 weeks a month
13	5		X(13)		X		X	X				X		X	X	Once (13)	Once (13)
16	3	X		X		X			X		X	Too young		X	X	Three times	1(16)
17	2	X			X	X			X		X		X	X	X	Never	Once/yr
20	7	X		X		Sometimes		X			X	No difference		X	X	Twice	Once/yr
21	3	X		X		X					Possibly		X	X	X	Once	Once
23	10		X(23)	X		X			X		X		X	X	X	Once	Never
24	10	X			X	X			X		X		X	X	X	Once	Twice/week (24)
25	4	X		X		Sometimes			X		X		X	X	X	Once	Twice
Total: 15	6.4 (average)	11 Yes	4 No	8 Yes	7 No	10 Yes · 2 Sometimes · 3 No		6 Yes · 7 No · 2 Q.n.a.		7 No · 4 Q.n.a. · 3 Yes · 1 Possibly		3 Presents · 10 Absents · 1 No difference · 1 Child is too young		14	14	6 Never · 5 Once · 2 Twice · 1 Three times	9 Once · 1 Never · 1 Twice · 3 Frequently

(3): He wasn't working.
(4): Even if he did not have regular work.
(7): Only when he stole.
(10): When he was working.
(13): He never worked.
(23): As he wasn't working, just before his imprisonment.
(1), (13), and (16): For moving or change of address.
(24): Or sometimes, three or four times a month only, wife and children sick.

Strangely enough, of the women who were working before their marriage, only one of the fifteen mothers questioned continued after the birth of their children. It is possible that the reason for this is that the women, who are all on welfare, are afraid of having it discontinued if they take a job. The interviews conducted in the homes seem to confirm this. Not only did the interviewers find them at home when they called, but in their notes they kept track of all the preliminary telephone conversations made during working hours.

In addition, many seemed to be ill, asthmatic, depressed, or said they hardly ever went out except to visit the prison or shop in the neighborhood.

The regard to attitudes, the first important fact is that the common-law wives of the prisoners did not seem to consider their husbands victims of society, but either weak men (six out of fifteen) or strong and superior (four out of fifteen). Of the fifteen families, six try to hide the fact from the children that their father, or the man replacing him, is in prison, but thirteen of the women visit their mates in prison.

The question of where the children live seems rather confusing. Of the fifteen respondents, thirteen stated that the children live with them, but the information concerning temporary placements, more or less prolonged, contradicts these answers and is further confirmed in the reports of the interviews. A similar finding applies to the answers of the women concerning their children's school situations and their scholastic results; these seem to be even more unsatisfactory according to the interviews than they appeared on the questionnaire, ever though the latter was filled out during the same meeting with the interviewer. In addition, six of the fifteen families admitted that the children had already had contact with the police.

We find, then, that the prisoners' common-law wives, although they attached no importance to the transmission of religious values and certain traditions (since none of the fifteen attended church and only three tried to justify this, two went to midnight mass at Christmas, and two said they had not been this year), were nonetheless anxious to show their interest in their children's progress in school.

Is this interest real or merely a manifestation of their fear that the social services will intervene and possibly place the children outside the home? I now present the reports of the interviews, if only to give a better idea of the complexity of the family ties and the conditions surrounding the relationships that exist between the parents and the children.

Reports of the Interviews with the Prisoners' Families

Family No. 1:

Common-law wife: She comes from the country; her parents did not have a farm, but they raised animals. She never criticizes her living companion. She has little contact with his mother.

The prisoner: He comes from the country. He would like to live in the country. His mother lives in Montreal with his youngest daughter, aged eighteen, who has stopped working; she sometimes used to go to look after the children, but for sometime now the eldest has been taking care of them. When he is at home, he works: he is a jack-of-all-trades.

Comments: Apartment quite large and very clean, although fairly old. Decorated for Chirstmas on November 29.

Family No. 2:

Common-law wife: She comes from the country; her parents still live there. Her husband and her living companion (the inmate) also come from the country. She brought up her young brother because her mother was working; he is living with her now and works in a warehouse.

Her husband: He is a day laborer who used to work here and there and is no longer working. It is she who looks after their three children, and they see their father often. The eldest thinks it better that his father is in prison than that he do what he does. He was just brought to court the day of the interview; he drinks a great deal and is sent to prison repeatedly (15 days to 1 month). She sees his parents occasionally.

Her living companion (the prisoner): He does not drink, but does not work, although he could do so since he knows mechanics and is good with his hands. His wife no longer wants him. She wants to remarry (a friend). She looks after the children, who do not know their father is in prison. Her living companion (prisoner) is the brother of his common-law wife's sister-in-law. They met at a family reunion. She knew that he had been in prison (1964) before coming to live with him. During their first year together, she placed her children with her sister and lived alone with him; she was working and went to see her children at night and on weekends. They lacked nothing since she sometimes earned up to $350 a week (barmaid); she never neglected them. She also attends to her living companion's children and brings them presents on their birthdays because that is what he would do if he were free. She got permission from Parthenais for him to go for a few minutes to the funeral parlor when his mother died (he came, handcuffed and between two guards). She says she can find him work on his release from prison. She is also prepared to work, but he does not want her to (jealous). He was once manager of a company in Winnipeg.

Miscellaneous: She does not talk to the neighbors and therefore has no problem concerning the fact that her friend is in prison; her children's friends do not know either. She owns a car.

Comments: Apartment clean. Quite well furnished. There are picture frames and boxes everywhere, which the prisoner had made in prison.

Family No. 4:

The wife: She is an only daughter, and both she and her husband come from the city. She is twenty-nine, and neurotic. She is in the care of a psychiatrist. She has no authority over the children, even those of three and four. She herself went to a judge to ask to have her children placed elsewhere, because she beats them. She asked that they be placed temporarily because she wants to take them back as soon as her husband gets out of prison. The first social worker on the case found a housekeeper for her. The worker who replaced the first one refused to supply one.

She worked as a waitress for 3 weeks last July, but had to stop because she used to faint.

She does not like the fact that her husband drinks, and she does not want to have anything to do with her husband's family.

Her mother works full time.

The children: The eldest (seven) was placed in the Centre d'accueil du Perpétuel Secours 7 weeks ago by the Social Welfare Service. He had just spent his first weekend at home: his mother finds him improved and more polite than usual. He likes living at the center; he plays hockey there. Before he was placed, he was very hard on his mother: "he even defecated on her." Ever since his father went to prison, he has not wanted to go to school. Before his father went away, he was an average pupil, but since that time, he spends most of his time "woolgathering." He used to say it was his mother's fault that his father left. He used to send his father drawings, and his father would send some back to him. He used to have asthma attacks when he was younger. His mother says he has never been in trouble with the police or appeared before a judge.

The other two children will be placed as soon as a foster home is found for them. The little girl of four has had bronchitis for the past 2 years.

Comments: She was in the process of painting the kitchen. She was smoking and crying. Her apartment is not arranged yet because she just moved in a month ago. There is not much furniture—only the strict necessities. Poor, but she was wearing a gold watch. She showed us photographs of her children. She says she will sleep a lot when her children are all placed.

Family No. 7:

Wife: She has been divorced from the prisoner since 1972 and has not seen him for a year. She now lives with her boyfriend and his two brothers. He has been working for 26 years. They say they love each other, but do not want to get married. They often have discussions; they understand one another. He comes from the Gaspé. She likes her work and is in good health (during the latter years of her marriage, she suffered a great deal from asthma). She says she has the right to reestablish her life; she did everything she could to help her husband (and can do no more). She wanted to "get him out of the mess" by paying his debts, and she paid some even after their divorce because she had signed for him.

Her mother and father both worked. She used to look after her brothers and sisters and went to night school. She used to make peace between her father and mother when they quarreled. Her mother was very strict; her father not at all. Today her parents live in the same house, but they each have their own entrance and their own side of the house. However, they eat at the same table. It was her parents who helped her get over her divorce.

She and her boy friend stopped drinking 4 months ago.

The prisoner: He is now in a detoxification center for drug addicts after having spent 6 or 7 months in prison. He was an alcoholic; he used to buy beer instead of food and would arrive home drunk; she could not put up with this. He did not like to work and was kept by her. He was very easily influenced. He had moments of great lucidity, alternating with moments of confusion. He took no interest in the children. One day he arrived at the house with two friends and threw a packet of stolen money at her: "You wanted money, now you have it." He gave her a violent beating in 1972. The cause of his criminality: weakness of character and his environment. She insists that with character, one can overcome any kind of milieu. They knew each other only 3 months when they got married. She says she had three children when she married in 1969; the prisoner says he had two, one seven and one ten years' old. She says she does not regret the experience because now she has learned her lesson. The prisoner's mother cannot help him because she is ill and on welfare.

The children: They have been living with their maternal grandparents since last July; their mother finds it hard to work and look after them. She wants to take them back a little later on when her own mother can no longer take care of them. The little girl of eight was deeply traumatized when she saw her father beat her mother: she was 10 days in an oxygen tent. She still remembers the scene. Toward the end of the marriage, she became asthmatic (a nervous state); now she is perfectly well. At the time, the doctors wanted to have her treated at the Institut Albert Prévost (she was four years old). They said that since the child's health depended on that of her mother, they wanted to treat the mother, but all she wanted was to be separated from her husband; after the separation, neither the mother nor the child needed any treatment. The boy (eleven or twelve) played hockey for 3 years, but is now too big to continue. He has been doing karate since September.

Comments: Middle class. Apartment well furnished.

Family No. 8:

Common-law wife: She is divorced. A native of the Gaspé, she was sixteen or seventeen when her parents moved to Montreal (her parents have since returned to the Gaspé). She would like to live in the country. Her husband is from the city, her boyfriend (the prisoner) as well. She had a dry-cleaning store, but dropped everything at the time of her divorce: too many responsibilities. The child was seven years old, and she had to get him up at six o'clock in the morning in order to open the store. It was difficult and she does not want to repeat the experience.

Comments: A most luxurious apartment, well set up. The woman was pretty, wore makeup, was very nice, was wearing several rings.

Family No. 9:

The wife: She comes from the Gaspé and has been living in Montreal 8 years, that is, since the birth of her child. Her father was a foreman and her mother a charwoman. They still live in the Gaspé. She has a brother in Montreal and babysits for him, but she cannot count on him for help. She is thinking of returning to her parents' home, but her husband does not want to, and she is afraid of him. Her social welfare allowance is not sufficient; she would like to work "under the table." A neighbor helps her.

She is in great fear of her husband (the prisoner) when he is drunk: "It takes four men to restrain him. . . ." At such times, he is capable of doing anything. He has threatened to kill her if she ever left him, and she believes he could do it, for every time he has said "she would be sorry for something," she has regretted it. Besides, he keeps weapons. She fears him "enough to have caused a depression." Several months before his present imprisonment, she was so afraid to go to sleep at night lest she never wake up that she used to leave with the children in the middle of the night. She once left while he was in prison for the weekend, and for a month and a half, he did not know where she was. She cannot count on her husband's family.

The prisoner: The eldest of a family of seven children, "a mama's boy." "He was unusually lucky. . . ." His father is now working at James Bay. He is a heavy drinker, but is not as violent as the prisoner. One of his brothers is like him.

His mother sends him money in prison. She spoiled him and brought him up badly. Among other things, she used to give him money for liquor. She does not want his wife to annoy him. The relationship between the two women has improved since his imprisonment. She and his father believe he will change.

He was carrying a loaded revolver when arrested the time before last. He has pals to whom he can never say no; they drink together. Then he does not go to work for 3 or 4 days. When he is drunk, he beats his wife. He never beats the children. He breaks everything. She had already laid a complaint against him in court because he had beaten her. He is jealous, but would allow her to work outside the house.

He has been unbearable for the past 6 years. He also takes drugs. He comes from the same small village in the Gaspé that she does. His parents live in Montreal.

The children: The oldest is eight years old and is repeating first year; he is above average. He failed his last year because they moved; she did not send him to school after the move because she did not know the new neighborhood. His father's behavior also upset him during this time; the child did not want his mother to drive his father away (he was 3 months without drinking). He loves his father; they play together for hours. When the father does not drink, he is very good to his children. The eldest child thinks his father is in the hospital. Last year, he told his father that he did not want to see him anymore when he drinks because he was afraid of him. The father has had contact with the police several times; the mother calls the police when the prisoner is drunk, breaks everything in the house, and beats her. The third child is an epileptic (a gland, they say; will perhaps operate when she is four years old). When she has an epileptic seizure, her right side becomes paralyzed. She has to take three pills a day, and even with her medication she can still have seizures.

One day when her husband was drunk, he threw a chair at the refrigerator. It bounced off and hit the second child on the head. She had to be taken to the hospital. The doctors considered it a case of a battered child and did not want to let her return to the house. The mother had had to explain that her husband had not done it on purpose and that he never beat the children. She gave birth to her third child that night.

She stays with her husband because of the children and because she is afraid he will carry out his threats. She is fine when he is not at home; she has more trouble with the children when he is there; and she is tired of having to support him.

Comments: The wife is obese and seems very motherly. The apartment is very clean (the little girl of two told us to remove our boots), cheerful, and well furnished, situated in a block of flats in Montreal East, a residential district near the river.

Family No. 10:

Mother of the prisoner: She comes from the Gaspé; they are going back in July with the children. They have been in Montreal 9 years, but have never become accustomed to living here: "The life is too fast." She suffers from chronic bronchitis (she rales), and she has not got the willpower to stop smoking. She has never worked outside the house. She does not always get along well with her daughter-in-law. She sends $20 a week to her son (the prisoner).

She has seven children. She brought up six of them. The other (the prisoner) was brought up by his grandmother because his mother was ill when he was born. His grandmother therefore looked after him and brought him up. She goes less often to church, which has "become a sort of discotheque," and attends midnight mass on television.

Father of the prisoner: A native of the Gaspé, he has always worked. He has been at James Bay since September 1977 (an operator of heavy machinery). He did not work outside Montreal for 17 years, but he earned only $200 a week, which was not enough to support five people. His wife thinks he has nerves of steel, but is a drunkard even though he never maltreats his family and has always succeeded in providing for them. She says she rested during the first 3 months he was in James Bay, then he came home for Christmas. When he was in Montreal, he never went out, but spent the day drinking, as usual.

Nevertheless, her husband has never stolen and has never gone to prison. He is fifty-one years old, is a strong man, and is very unhappy that his son is in prison. At Christmas, he went to the prison to see the prisoner and cried when he saw inmates who had not received one visit.

Sister of seventeen: She goes to see her brother in prison and brings him money sent by his mother. She has left school and is of the opinion that everyone there smokes pot, not to speak of the case of beer under the table at the cafeteria.

She is a quiet girl who does not go out except with her mother and has a boyfriend who is still going to school. She worked twice in a drugstore, but is not working at the moment.

Brother of fifteen: He is not good at school: "It's lucky he is good at hockey." He plays on the bantam team. Last year he went to a prep school, but he was expelled. This year he is not going to school. His mother wants to try and convince him to go back.

Brother of thirteen: He plays in a hockey club. He would be brilliant in school, but he is very "difficult." He made a painting that hangs on the wall.

Other children: The second oldest does not drink because he "becomes aggressive" as soon as he drinks a bottle of beer. The third (twenty-three years old) drinks heavily, but has no problem with the law.

A girl of twenty-six who has two children lives nearby. She will probably go back to the Gaspé when her parents go.

The Prisoner: He is the oldest of seven children. Because his mother was ill, his maternal grandmother looked after him from the time he was 3 months old, and he lived with her until the age of fourteen. He was "extremely spoiled," especially by his grandfather who was an invalid. He was very brilliant in school. Always came first in class even though he never did any homework. The nuns (teachers) used to come to the house to congratulate his parents. He got an excellent school report, which his mother still keeps. He left school in nineth grade. He liked school, but belonged to a gang. He was very hardworking. He has the best heart of all the family. He is good to his children. He is not a drunkard. He can go for a month without drinking. He is a good chap. He is proud and likes things to be in order. His problem is that he cannot say no and has no will of his own. His mother says she cannot understand him and finds him uncommunicative. He does not talk. He was allowed home for 3 days at Christmas and 3 days at the New Year. He cried when he had to return to prison. While in detention he does crafts and brought his mother a lovely lamp for Christmas.

According to his mother, his behavior is not due to her or her husband. His brothers and sisters go to see him in prison, but the mother does not have the courage to go. According to her, the family has always been close, and she cites, as an example, the fact that they often play cards together. In her opinion, her son has "unfortunately not been in prison long enough to become reformed."

Wife of the prisoner: According to the prisoner's mother, the wife is a good woman who looks after her husband and children, but does not encourage him. She treats him like a dirty dog. When he buys her something, she sells it a week later. In the last 6 months, however, she has improved, for she washes her dishes; all the same, she continued to swear and run him down, and this discourages her husband. The prisoner's delinquency could be caused to a certain extent by his family problems. His mother says she cannot go along with a wife who "discourages" her husband.

Family No. 11:

Mother of the prisoner's common-law wife: A native of Pointe-aux Trembles, which was a rural area at the time, at the age of two, she lost her six brothers and sisters during the 1918 epidemic of Spanish influenza. Her grandmother looked after her until she was eight, when her grandfather died, and she was placed in an orphanage where she spent 3 years in the novices' quarters. At nineteen she married a friend of the family. Her husband always worked, was a strong man, and did not drink. Eleven years ago he had a heart attack at work. She was therefore obliged to look for a job. She used to work all morning, come home to prepare the lunch, work all afternoon, come home to prepare the supper, and then return to clean offices until two o'clock in the morning; she fell ill with meningitis in 1972. She was in a coma for 2 months and after that was forced to ask for welfare. She had six children, but raised only the two youngest, one being the common-law wife of the prisoner.

The prisoner's common-law wife: She always had a weakness for bums. At the age of twelve she belonged to a gang whose members were always in juvenile court, but she herself was never there. Her mother used to put her in the corner. According to her brother, most of the young people in the neighborhood where they lived went to juvenile court.

When she was seventeen, her mother could no longer talk to her and asked her to go to work or leave. The young girl therefore decided to live with a man who had been in prison. Her mother called the Juvenile Aid Services, but they answered that she could not stop her daughter from living with a man, nor from having a baby, if she wanted.

The prisoner's common-law wife is now twenty-three, and in her mother's opinion, she would rather starve than work. According to the mother, her daughter and the prisoner are lazy and irresponsible. When they do not call her, it is because all is going well and they do not need money. However, if they call, usually it is to ask for something, although they receive as much money from social welfare as she does, and she has to pay for her medicines. Her daughter has an allowance of $480 a month for her and her two children, and her rent is only $190.

The grandchildren: The mother of the prisoner's common-law wife buys clothes for her grandchildren. They do not know their father is in prison; they think he is at James Bay. The children seem to be treated well, but they will never be hardworking, for they see that their father and mother are good-for-nothings. The prisoner and her daughter (his common-law wife) want to have two children because the two they are bringing up are from another union; the first is the child of the wife and her first living companion and the second is that of the prisoner and another woman.

The prisoner: According to the mother of his common-law wife and her brother, he is a good chap, but perhaps was not brought up properly. He was thrown out of the house at age fourteen and went to live with his grandmother. He has worked before, but in fits and starts, and it never lasts long. He drinks a lot. He would like to make a new start, but it is difficult with a criminal record, because as soon as an employer learns about it, he is fired. He is out of prison at the moment, but is not working.

According to the mother of his common-law wife, he has always lived on welfare. When the couple was living with her, a job was found for him at a carwash, but he was unable to keep it. He has never kept a job more than a month.

He has worked in all the garages in the neighborhood and was so "lazy" that he used to take the bus to go two blocks.

Comments: The mother of the common-law wife had a boyfriend after her husband's death, but the children, and especially the two youngest, did not want her to remarry. The little girl used to answer the telephone, "You have the wrong number, Mr."

Family No. 12:

The prisoner's wife: She misses her husband a great deal, and it was hard when he went to prison. However, she knew he had already been in prison when she married him after going with him for a year. He was just out of prison when she met him, and his family accepted this, in a way, since her brothers-in-law also had spent time in prison.

She cannot work because of the children and receives just enough money from social welfare to exist on. She hopes her husband will not return to prison and will go to work when he gets out. She is very much alone in the meantime, for her parents do not understand the situation. In her own family no one has ever been sentenced to imprisonment.

The children: They are lonesome for their father when he is not there and talk to him on the telephone, but they do not cry. They think he is working outside Montreal.

Family No. 13:

The prisoner's common-law wife: Unmarried mother. Lives only for her son, aged four. A man is of little importance to her. She has moved to Montreal and knows absolutely no one. She never goes out.

She used to live in St. Jerome, where her parents still live. She is now living on a welfare allowance, which amounts to $357 a month for her and her child. Her rent is $155, so this is not sufficient for her needs. If she were working, however, she would not have more money, since she would have to pay a babysitter. Nonetheless, she has never inquired about the price of a day nursery or other such services. In any case, she would have to work in a factory or as a charwoman, which she has no wish to do.

The prisoner: Sentenced to 7 years in prison, he is not a good father according to his common-law wife, since he is a recidivist. He wants to resume living with her, but she wants to leave him. His rehabilitation is up to him alone, and even if she helps him, nothing would change. She wants him to work when he gets out of prison, but it will be difficult for him to find a job with a criminal record, particularly since he does not like to work. For the moment, he does crafts in prison and gives her his sculptures.

The child: He almost never goes out of the apartment. In St. Jerome, he used to go to nursery school, but in Montreal, his mother does not know the neighborhood and does not think it worthwhile looking for one just to send the child for 2 hours a day. The boy sleeps with his mother. He pays no attention to the women who come to the apartment, but when it is a man, he will climb up on his knee. He never hugs his mother, but hugs the prisoner, even when the latter is bad to his mother. The mother says that the child is her whole life, however, and that she will never leave him for a man.

Family No. 16:

Common-law wife: She sometimes smokes pot, because in her opinion, it is less harmful than tobacco. She never takes drugs, however, because of the child and because it is dangerous.

She still needs her mother, her advice and help. When her boyfriend is in prison, she spends 2 weeks a month with her mother, near Valleyfield. When she was a child, she and her sister were placed in a convent, where they lived for 2 years. After that, they were looked after at home by a maid. The maid used to entertain her "boyfriends" and leave the children outside, but their parents, who were both working, never knew this.

The prisoner: He has $7,000 worth of debts, contracted in order to ensure his defence during a trial on a charge of drug trafficking, which lasted 2 years.

After spending 8 months in prison, he will be out on parole and will go to work in James Bay, where his salary will be $350 a week. He has already lost two jobs because of the trial, but he does not allow himself to become downhearted, and he comforts her as much as he can.

At the age of fourteen or fifteen, he was at Boscoville[6] and St. Vallier,[7] from which he ran away. He lived in St. Henri, used to take part in street fights, and enjoys sports. At Boscoville, he gave physical education courses. The son of a family of ten children, where the eldest worked to provide for the younger ones, the prisoner gave his salary to his parents, who used it to entertain the neighbors. The children ate what was left when the guests had gone.

His father is black and his mother Italian. His mother was fifteen when her eldest girl was born. The child was always looked after by her grandmother. She has since been in prison.

For many years the prisoner looked after his twin brothers, who had left home. He does not take drugs, and he only wanted to sell some to make money. "Today you mustn't be honest in order to live; the laborer who works by the sweat of his brow gets nowhere."

The wife's projects: She has applied for work at James Bay. A former convict who works with her husband wants to help her get the job, but she wants to stay only a year and then never work again. Her mother will look after the child while she is away. When she comes back, she will buy a farm where she will keep horses, a pony for the child, and some cows. She would like to breed dogs and have a large garden.

The child: The little girl only started to walk at fourteen months, for there was not enough space in the apartment for her to do anything but crawl.

Family No. 17:

Wife of the prisoner: She goes out only to visit the prison. In the past, she worked in a hospital for children with cerebral palsy, but she does not want to work anymore.

The prisoner: His wife believes that he will not start up again. All that will be done with. What is serious is that he is always afraid that his family is in need, so when she visits him, she does not talk about her problems. Once she cried, and he did not like it at all.

The children: The youngest misses his father. He often cries in school, and he does so to such an extent that the prisoner wants his wife to tell the child's teacher about his imprisonment. She has more difficulty with the children since their father left. The eldest is very aggressive in school.

Miscellaneous: She does not speak to the neighbors. There is a coolness between her and her own family. Her father and mother accept her husband's imprisonment, but her brothers and sisters do not. She has more contact with her husband's family than with her own.

Family No. 20:

Wife of the prisoner: Her parents came from the country, but she and her brothers and sisters were brought up in Montreal. Her father is a carpenter. Her mother does not work.

The prisoner: His wife does not think that he will ever be a regular worker. He has "an artistic temperament" and could make a living as a sculptor, but his work is not the kind that appeals to the public.

The children: They have five children, and she is afraid that their father's influence will affect their future. Her daughters find her hard on them sometimes.

Comments: She has no prejudice against the legal system. It is the Crown Prosecutors duty to be inhuman, but the defense lawyers chosen by her husband are good, including the one from Legal Aid.

Family No. 21:

Wife of the prisoner: She has close ties with her family, who give her money, but no relationship with her husband's family. Her father always had a job, but he drank. Her mother never worked.

The prisoner: His wife hopes that he will become rehabilitated. True, his brothers are delinquents, but his family is not very close. She would like to talk to people and meet other prisoners' wives.

The children: Their mother does not think they will be affected by their father's imprisonment. She says she has always had difficulty with the children. The boy behaves differently since his father left. He misses him and often cries.

Family No. 23:

Wife of the prisoner: Her parents do not like her husband because he is in prison. She cut off all ties with her family a year ago. She keeps in touch with her husband's family, and her father-in-law, among others, comes to look after the children. She says she is resigned to the imprisonment of her husband and to being alone. She has applied for his parole and is waiting for the result. In the meantime, she goes out only to go to the grocery store and to the prison on Sunday.

When she married him, she knew he had been in prison, but she hoped he would change. She says she is strong, but he will not be released from prison for 2 more months and that's a long time. She feels very much alone and writes him every day.

The prisoner: His father used to beat his mother and the children. He nearly killed him on three occasions. He was almost always in prison. One night he went out to get the supper and came back 7 years later. His mother was extremely poor. They often went hungry. She used to drink a lot and go out a great deal. The children were left alone in the house. When he was a child, it was he who did the housework and looked after the others. When his mother would come home drunk in the middle of the night, she would wake him up. He brought himself up, for his parents never looked after him. His mother used to throw him out of the house. Between the ages of ten and fifteen, he spent 2 years away from home. He was living alone before his marriage. He does not want his children to be like him. He is a good father and is very lonesome for his children while in prison. He landed in prison because his family needed money, and he is paying dearly for his mistake.

He asked for a transfer to the Maison St-Laurent; he would start to work, but the woman who wants to hire him cannot guarantee the authorities the number of hours of work she could give him a week. She is a florist. In addition, she would buy handicrafts from him to sell in her store. He is very good at carpentry. In prison he makes wooden chests. He is just now making one for his wife.

The children: The second child recently underwent three ear, nose, and throat operations. The third child has asthma and had ten attacks last year; she had to be hospitalized. This year she has only had two attacks. She takes medication, but not every day. The eldest child is not the prisoner's child, but has no contact with his natural father.

Before her husband went to prison, this child did not attend school, but his mother was not aware of it; a social worker informed her of the fact. Since then, the child has returned to school, and the social worker is pleased with him. The social worker sees the child once a week. The second son is a good pupil and is joining the cadets this summer.

Both the prisoner's children are affected by their father's imprisonment and have problems both in and out of school. They almost never go outside to play.

Comments: The wife is short of money, and there is not enough heat. The apartment should have a large heating unit. At present, the apartment has only two small electric heaters, which are not sufficient. The wife pays $120 a month rent plus the electricity, and the owner makes no repairs. There is just enough money left for food. Hydro-Quebec cut off her electricity last week, and social welfare had to pay the bill. In future, therefore, $40 a month will be deducted from her check to pay for her electricity.

Family No. 24:

Prisoner's common-law wife: Her father was French, he married her mother just before the war and was killed in the army. She was told that he was a good man, but she does not know what his profession was. Her mother never worked, but received a pension from the army. She married again and had another daughter. Her second husband died of cancer when the baby, her half-sister, was a year and a half old. She was always a good mother, and still is. She keeps close ties with her mother and half-sister. She does not go out and cannot work because social welfare will stop sending her check. At the welfare office, moreover, they practically advised her to "become a streetwalker." She no longer believes in the church, since a parish priest refused to help her once when her check was stolen and she was consequently forced to place her children.

The first husband of the prisoner's common-law wife: Her first husband was always in court, but for minor infractions since he was in prison only a total of 2 months. He deserted her when she was in the hospital. He left with her best friend. He came to the house to see the children a month before Christmas with his common-law wife and their little girl of two or three years. About 9 months ago he had a motorcycle accident, and one side of his face is disfigured. He now receives a disability pension from social welfare.

The children: She had six, but lost three, two during pregnancy because of a state of nerves brought on by her husband's behavior. The third died at the age of two, struck by an automobile. She had given the child for adoption, and it was at the home of the adoptive parents that the accident occurred. The three children who live with her witnessed the arrest of her common-law husband. They asked afterward if he was a gangster and what he had to do with the police.

The children were present during the interview. The youngest boy said that he was sorry about the accident that happened to his "father" and that he still loved him (the mother's face hardened just then). He also said that he liked school, but that he was accused in class of causing trouble but it was not true.

The middle boy should be placed very soon. He does not want to study. He once set fire to the letter box in the apartment where they used to live. At the age of twelve, he is still in the first grade. According to his mother, he only goes to school in the afternoon, since his teachers can stand him only for half a day at a time. He had just arrived from school and said he was hungry, whereupon he was roundly scolded by his mother. She thinks you do not say things like that and said he would not dare do so if his father were home. He remarked to his mother that she was not usually dressed so early in the day. His remark was taken well and even corroborated. As for the fourteen-year-old girl, she behaved like a baby, but it seems that she drinks at "parties" and comes home drunk. At school she is under the supervision of the youth services.

The prisoner: He has not been in trouble for 5 years, that is, since the beginning of their relationship. The police caught up with him for a previous failure to appear following a warrant issued in 1972. His imprisonment is as hard on her as it is on him. She is sticking with him, no good or not. He is good to her. They get along well. She calls the prison very often to get permission for him to get out during various holidays. He loves the children and disciplines them. They "toe the line" when he is home, even though the police arrested him in front of them. They were not threatening, however, but told him that if he did not come along, they would go and get a warrant. In her opinion, her common-law husband was unlucky. The policemen changed their version depending on whether they were talking to the defense lawyer on the telephone or to the prisoner. The lawyer changed his mind as well. He was very bad at the trial and did not open his mouth.

The police told the prisoner that they were not taking him for long, but he was 3 weeks at the Parthenais Center and was then sentenced to 6 months. The police should have told him the truth or nothing at all; it would not have been so hard.

The wife was present at the trial; she is used to going because her first husband was "always being brought to court." Her husband had a good lawyer, but his friends at court advised him to take another. He pleaded guilty in order to get only 6 months, because they told him that if he pleased not guilty, he could get up to 2 years. He cried when he heard his sentence.

Family No. 25:

Wife of the prisoner: She comes from the Gaspé. She does not want to go back there or live in Montreal. Her father was a lumberman and an alcoholic. He drank away all his money, even though he earned a pretty good salary. He has been separated from her mother for 9 years. He lives in Ontario and she in Montreal, not far from her daughter. She was a teacher in the Gaspé before her marriage, and 4 years later she had to start working again because her husband did not bring home any money. She is now working in a hospital.

If the wife had no children, she would go to work, but she must look after them. She did not tell social welfare that her husband was in prison, for she knew a woman whose check was reduced by $50 a month when the service found out that her husband was in jail. In any case, 2 days after she receives her check, there is no money left. Fortunately, the corner store gives her credit, and the children never lack for food.

The prisoner: The charge for which he is now serving his sentence was endorsed by his brother, so that the prisoner was sentenced to only 3 months. In 7 years, that is, since their marriage, this is the first time he has gone to prison. He committed the crime because he needed money. He does not like always being "down to his last cent."

The children: The oldest ones often send drawings to their father. They miss him a great deal. The children cry on the telephone when their father calls them. They know he is in prison, but they tell their friends he is working outside the city.

The interviews show the basic realities much more clearly than the answers to the questionnaire: the common denominator for all the families is that they belong to a group. The criminality of the boyfriend, father, or foster father is not an isolated phenomenon, but frequently occurs in the wife's previous union or in the family of one or the other of the partners. These are factors which make the wife more permissive regarding her companion, but the question is whether this kind of permissiveness can have an influence on the values transmitted to the children.

Contrary to the images derived from the approach that crime is related to a spirit of adventure, the study of the prisoners and their families presents a rather limited panorama of the real potential of the men concerned. The women, who seem to be sufficiently attached to their partners to wait for their release from prison and to constantly hope for a change in the lot they share, more easily acknowledge their "sicknesses," such as alcoholism, the use of drugs, and so on, than their misdeeds. Although the women claim they have fewer problems with their children when the man is present than when he is in prison (ten out of fifteen) and the prisoners confirm this, the fact remains that in six families out of fifteen, an effort is made to hide the whereabouts of the fathers from the children.

Generally speaking, it seems possible to conclude that on the basis of all the answers obtained and the interviews held with both the prisoners and their companions, these couples do not seek to transmit countervalues to their children or the attitude that a criminal career is justified by the shortcomings of society, thus affording a possible excuse for delinquency.

In short, the group cannot be considered consciously criminogenic, but given the kind of existence these people lead, the transmission of certain habits and deviant behavior is almost automatic. The women's attachment to the prisoners, unjustified as it may be in itself, is an element of stability in the relationship of the couple and theoretically an important factor in helping the prisoners to overcome the depression caused by the isolation of the prison. This does not mean that it necessarily ensures the social reintegration of the men; however, it is always a disturbing element in the development of the children. Although it is practically impossible to prove on the basis of my research, we may well ask whether the fact that some of the women disappear with their children, leaving no trace for their husbands or living companions, is not proof that there is a desire, greater than this attachment, to protect the children from the vicious circle of criminality.

Whatever the case, I finish this analysis of the families of prisoners with a report of statements made regarding the relations of the prisoners with those of their children who have reached or passed the age of legal majority.

The average number of children in the prisoners' families is 3.3, and their average age is 10.4. In the group, there are very young children, babies, some of school age, and some who work. Some of the children are the offspring of a first union of the prisoner, others that of his common-law wife. I do not believe it possible to measure the variables in the evolution of the natural and legitimate children, the first and second born; I simply indicate the situation of the eldest, according to the opinion expressed by the prisoners concerned and what they themselves told us during the interviews.

Prisoner No. 5: According to the prisoner, the fact that he is in prison can have no influence on his son. Yet the latter recently spent a weekend in the police station for receipt of an automobile that his cousin had stolen.

Prisoner No. 15: The prisoner has four children, one a girl of seventeen who has been in the hospital since his imprisonment. She had an attack a year before the prisoner was arrested, perhaps a result of drugs. At the time, she spent 3 months at the Y. Institute. Another of his children is hospitalized because of a state of depression (twenty years old). The other two, fifteen and nineteen, respectively, are "fine."

Prisoner No. 19: His son of twenty-three is serving a sentence at Bordeaux at the same time as he. He once got 18 months for a hold-up he committed on impulse, and his father threw him out of the house. Before that, he used to steal from his father and had no respect for his mother. At nineteen he was sentenced to 2 years in the penitentiary for the theft of an automobile. He left school when he was about thirteen, while his father was in prison. He was often transferred from one school to another. His mother placed him with his paternal grandmother when he was thirteen; he was not stealing at the time, but he lacked respect for his mother and would come home late at night. His father does not think he was ever at the Social Welfare Court, but he is not sure. "The child's delinquency comes from the fact that his father was involved in crime." Now his father talks to him and has convinced him to take an interest in the hotel and never go back to prison. The other two children are very good. The boy of eighteen works at the hotel, as does the girl, who works there as a barmaid. These two children were younger and did not know their father was in prison; they thought he was in the hospital. They have always lived with their mother and were not marked by their parents' problems.

Prisoner No. 26: His son sometimes takes drugs; he became very lazy, liking to smoke hash. However, he respects his parents. He left school at sixteen.

Thus in both cultures, French and English, based on the interviews and answers to the questionnaire, the prisoners seem to be very concerned about the future of their children. They are aware, although they do not say it in so many words, that neither they nor their companions give their children the values necessary for them to develop properly in society. They remember their own childhood and want to avoid the same fate for their children, but this is only an abstract wish, similar to the vows they make that when they get out of prison they will not start their old habits again—pledges their criminal records systematically contradict.

**Families of Female Prisoners and Symbols of
the Maternal Image**

Women Prisoners and Their Families

When the files for my research were selected in February 1978, the total population of Maison Tanguay fluctuated between sixty and seventy prisoners.

On February 6, 1978, there were seventy-four inmates. As in the case of the men. I did not count prisoners awaiting trial and those given intermittent sentences.

Contrary to the prisoners at the Montreal Detention Center, however, this group's criminal records showed more serious crimes, not necessarily connected with recidivism, as in the case of the men, for which the sentences were sometimes of longer duration, including life.

According to an agreement between the federal and provincial prison administrations, Quebec prisons, and in particular the Maison Tanguay, receive women sentenced to more than 2 years. This was arranged so that they would not have to serve their sentences in an Anglophone milieu, far from their families. Otherwise they would theoretically have to be sent to Kingston Penitentiary, the only prison that has a section for women prisoners.

The list of prisoners who stated on their admission forms that they had children of their own or in their care included thirty names, or about 50 percent of the total population. Of these thirty, some were released at the time I was starting the first interviews, others were working on the outside during the day and were not available, and one refused to answer my questions. Consequently, the group of prisoners studied comprised only twenty-two women.

The interviews took place in private visiting areas in the prison, small rooms containing several chairs and sometimes a table. Every morning we would fill in a form containing the list of prisoners to be seen during the day, making several copies for the secretariat. The inmates were brought in one by one, and the interviewer was left alone with the prisoner.

Unlike the men, the women prisoners were afraid that we wanted to meet their children in order to take them away. One of them said that she had killed her husband because he had tried to take her children from her and that she would do the same again to protect them, if necessary.

The fact is, however, that in the majority of cases the prisoners' children were placed in foster homes. I might add that since the Maison Tanguay receives prisoners from various parts of the country, unlike the Bordeaux Detention Center, where most come from Montreal and its suburbs, many of the prisoners' families live far away.

There is also a marked difference in the way the male prisoners and the female prisoners regard the crimes they have committed. For the male prisoners questioned it was always "the last time." They said they now "understood" and intended to change their way of life. The women, on the other hand, seemed convinced that they were born criminals, despite the fact that very often they were serving their first sentence.

In general, the interviews with the women prisoners lasted longer than those with the men. Having relatively more frequent contacts with social workers, at least inside the prison, the women prisoners seemed more suspicious and would not easily confide in the interviewer.

All these constraints made it necessary for us to reformulate the question-naire so that the women prisoners could also answer the questions which, in the case of the men, were put to their families. Tables 3-11 through 3-19 were compiled in the same way as for the men, showing the results obtained through study of the records and the answers to the questionnaire and interviews, which lasted an average of over an hour. For reasons of confidentiality, the names of the prisoners are replaced by numbers from 27, proceeding from the last number given the men, to 48. Hence the cases of twenty-two prisoners are presented.

The findings obtained from the answers shown in the tables are in them-selves interesting, but even more significant when compared with those of the men prisoners.

First of all, as I have said, although the nature of the crimes committed and the duration of the sentences are not the same for the men and women prisoners concerned, their ages vary from twenty-five to forty-six, with the exception of three women, twenty one (No. 31), twenty-two (No. 42), and twenty-three (No. 48), respectively. Despite the smaller number of female delinquents (twenty-two women to twenty-six men), the prisoners in both groups are of comparable age, although a few of the women are younger. In all cases, however, the prisoners are men and women who have reached the age of maturity. The same holds true for the mates of the prisoners, as shown in the tables of the prisoners' families, where, with the exception of one com-mon-law wife, all the others gave ages varying from twenty-four to forty.

The questions designed to find out the male prisoners' aspirations in terms of an occupation, job, or trade (What trade would you like to practice?) were answered more with a view of confirming what they had already told the administration, or to making a joke, than to stating a dream or an ambition. Thus of twenty-six men respondents, the majority mention the same trade they were practicing before their detention, even though many of them answered negatively to the question "Did you work half time or full time before your imprisonment."

One prisoner of the twenty-six said he was a chauffeur and would like to have been a fireman, another that he would have liked to become an elec-tronics specialist, and a third that he would be interested in a career in music. Two of the men, with a wry sense of humor, said they would like to become a prison director and a gambler, respectively.

It seems that women prisoners, on the other hand, have more ambition. They stated that they would have liked to be a dancer, a veterinarian, a hair-dresser, an artist, or a journalist. They show a certain optimism, for neither their past, their present, nor their age seems to be considered a hindrance, as evidenced by the woman of forty-six who said she was a saleslady and would like to become a journalist.

Table 3-11
Questionnaire Administered to Female Prisoners: Profile of the Prisoners

No.	Age	Marital Status	Profession	What Trade Would You Have Liked to Practice?	Before Entering Prison, Did You Have a Job?				Type of Work?
					Full Time		Part Time		
					Yes	No	Yes	No	
27	38	Div., clw[a]	Housekeeper	Office work		X		X	Cashier, saleswoman, etc.
28	35	Separated	Dressmaker	Dressmaker		X		X	
29	26	Separated		Dancer		X		X	
30	32	Widow, clw	Housekeeper	Work in a private home		X		X	
31	21	Unmarried	Housekeeper	Secretary		X		X	Waitress
32	26	Unmarried	Nurses's aid, etc.	Veterinary	X			X	L.I.P. project[b]
33	31	Married	Mother of a family	Doesn't want to work		X		X	
34	46	Married	Saleswoman	Journalist	X			X	Saleswoman
35	28	Married		Hairdresser		X		X	Hairdresser
36	36	Divorced	Secretary	Social worker		X		X	
37	31	Div. mar.		Question not asked	X			X	Barmaid
38	29	Unmarried		Any job		X		X	
39	38	Separated	Barmaid	Nurse's aid		X		X	Waitress
40	34	Unmarried		Art		X		X	
41	36	Sep., clw	Waitress	Waitress		X		X	
42	22	Unmarried	Housekeeper	In a private home		X		X	In a private home
43	26	Unmarried	Post Office	Painter	X		X		Barmaid
44	39	Separated		Doesn't know		X		X	
45	30	Married		Nurse's aid		X	X		Secretary
46	42	Divorced	Artist	Electronics		X	X		Artist
47	26	Married		Journalist		X	X		Receptionist
48	23	Married		Cameraman	X			X	Camera Technician
Total: 22	31.6				5	17	4	18	

6 Married
6 Unmarried
4 Separated
2 Divorced
1 Widow, clw; 1 div., clw; 1 sep., clw; 1 div., remarried

Table 3-11 continued

No.	If You Had the Choice, Would You Rather Live in the City (Cit.) or the Country (C)?	Have You Often Moved from One Region of the Province to Another?		In Prison, What Activities Do You Participate In?[c]
		Yes	No	
27	Cit.		X	A,C,D[c]
28	C	Always		A,C,D, theater
29	C	Once		A,D
30	C		X	A,C
31	Both	Twice		A,C
32	C	Twice		D,E, she writes
33	C	X		B,C,D (at one time E)
34	Both			C,D,E, theatre
35	Cit.		X	A,B,C,E
36	C	Once		C,D
37	—	Q.N.A.		C,D
38	C		X	A,B,D
39	Cit.		X	A,B,C,D,E
40	C		X	B,C,D
41	Both	X		A,B,C (at one time E)
42	C	X		A,B,C,D
43	Cit.	X		A,B,C,D,E
44	Cit.		X	A,D
45	C		X	A,B,C,D,E
46	C	X		B,C,D
47	C	X		A,B,C,D (at one time E)
48	Cit.		X	B,D, theater
Total: 22	7 In the city 11 In the country 3 Both 1 Q.n.a.	11 1 Q.n.a.	10	A 14 D 18 B 12 E 6 and 3 used to C 17 participate

[a]Common-law wife

[b]Local Initiatives Program

[c]A = television, radio; B = sports; C = manual work other than what is obligatory; D = reading; E = prisoners' committee.

Table 3-12
Questionnaire Administered to Female Prisoners: "Did You Live With...?"

No.	Your Parents? Yes	Your Parents? No	Until What Age?	Your Mother Yes	Your Mother No	Was She Working? Yes	Was She Working? No	Type of Work	Is Your Mother Alive? Yes	Is Your Mother Alive? No	Your Father Yes	Your Father No	Did He Work? Yes	Did He Work? No
27	X		18	X			X		X		X		X	
28	X		10	X		X		Owner of apart. building		X	X		X	
29	X		21	X			X			X	X		X	
30	X		18	X			X			X	X		X	
31	X		13	X			X			X	X		X	
32	X		19	X		X				X	X		X	
33	X		15	X			X		X		X		X	
34	X		16	X		X		In a restaurant		X	X		X	
35	X		16	X		X		Nurse		X	X		X	
36	X		21	X			X		X		X		X	
37	X (adoptive)		14	X			X		X		X (adoptive)		X	
38	X		14	X			X			X	X		X	
39	X		16	X			X			X	X		X	
40	X		14	X			X			X	X		X	
41	X		4	X		X		Waitress		X		X		Doesn't know
42	X		6	X		X		Dressmaker		X	X		X	
43	X		15	X			X			X	X		X	
44	X		15	X			X		X		X		X	
45	X		18	X			X			X	X		X	
46	X		11	X		X		Ballet dancer	X		X		X	
47	X		17	X			X			X	X		X	
48	X		17	X		X		Sells antiques		X	X		X	
Total: 22	22		14.9	22		8	14		6	16	21	1	20	1 Q.n.a. 1 ?

Table 3-12 continued

No.	Type of Work	Is He Living? Yes	Is He Living? No	Your Husband?	How Many Years?	Was He Working? Yes	Was He Working? No	Type of Work	Age	Your Children? Yes	Your Children? No
27	Lumberman and handyman		X	X	11	X		Handyman	42	X	
28	Construction	X		X	9	X		Electrician	—	X	
29	Agronomist		X	X	5	X		Labourer	31	X	
30	Miner	X		X	4	X		Miner	—	X	
31	Construction	X								X	
32	Businessman		X								X
33	Hotelkeeper	X		X	16		X	None	34	X	
34	Carpenter	X		X	29	X		Designer	—	X	
35	Train		X	X	12	X		Shipper	35	X	
36	Prospecter	X		X (2 husbands)	2	X		Bookkeeper	—	X (36)	
37	—	X		X		X				X	
38	Coal		X							X	
39	Lumberman		X	X	2	X		Boxer	28	X	
40	Handyman		X							X	
41	Mechanic	Doesn't know		X	2	X		Driver	61	X (41)	
42	Miner		X							X	
43	Autowash	X								X	
44	Construction	X		X	3 months	X		Upholsterer	39	X	
45	Postman		X	X	5	X		Bookkeeper	28	X	
46	Manufacturer	X		X	4	X		Engineer	—	X	
47	Manufacturer		X	X	9	X		Artist	29	X	
48	Radio Broadcaster		X	X	4	X		Carpenter	26	X	
Total 22:		10 1?	11	16 NB: 6 are unmarried	7.6	15	1		35.3	21 (36): One out of four (41): Sometimes	1

Table 3-12 continued

No.	Your Living Companion?	For How Many Years?	Was He Working? Yes	Was He Working? No	Type of Work	Person to Notify in Case of Emergency
27	X	2	X		Chauffeur truck	Sister
28	X (8)	9 altogether	X		Technician, etc.	Companion
29						Father
30	X	10		X	Miner	Father-in-law
31	X	3	X		Cook	Girlfriend
32						Father
33						No one
34						Husband
35						Father
36	X (2)	8 total	1st	2nd	House painter	Friend
37						Friend
38	X	5	X		Manufacturer	Mother
39						Husband and brother
40	X (2)	13 total	2nd	1st	Lumberman	Daughter
41	X (several)		X		Decorator, moneylender	Mother
42	X (2)	9 total	1st	2nd	Musician	Father
43	X (2)	5 total	1st	2nd	Musician, agent	Companion
44	X	10	X		Truckdriver	Daughter
45						Mother
46	X	9	X		Salesman or farmer	No one
47						Father and mother
48						Husband
Total: 22	12		7	1		4 fathers; 3 mothers; 2 friends; 3 husbands; 2 daughters; 1 friend; 2 companions; 2 no one; 1 sister

The numeral in parentheses shows the number of living companions.

4 Yes for the one, no for the other

Table 3-13
Questionnaire Administered to Female Prisoners: Prisoners' Children

No.	No. of Persons in Prisoner's Care	No. of Children	What Ages?	Who Are They Living with at Present?	Who Supports Them?		
					The Social Service	Their Father	Other
27	1	4	18, 15, 14, 8	1: apt		X	
28	0	4	18, 16, 15, 13	Father		X	
29	1	1	5	A family		X	
30	1	2	10, 4	1: foster home; 1: father	1	1	
31	1	1 (p)[a]	2	Mother of her companion			
32	1	1	6	Maternal grandparents		X	
33	4	4	16, 15, 13, 11	2: foster homes; 2: with friends	X		Grandparents
34	1	5	28, 25, 23, 20, 13	2: father; 3: apt.			1 and 4 are self-supporting
35	2	2	11, 5	Father		X	
36	2	4 (p)	15, 11, 8, 2	2: adopted; 2: foster homes			
37	1	1	7	Foster home	X		
38	–	4	14, 13, 10, 9	Maternal grandmother	X		
39	1	1	12	Girlfriend			Child welfare
40	4	4	17, 16, 15, 12	Group home	X		
41	5	5	18, 17, 14, 11, 8	1: father; 2: foster homes; 2: being adopted	50% and 50%		
43	1	2	8, 4	1: foster home; 1: adopted	X		
44	1	3	22, 21, 18	Apt.			Self-supporting
45	1	1	8	Maternal grandparents			The prisoner
46	0	3	21, 19, 17	Apt.			Self-supporting
47	–	1	8	Maternal grandmother		X and grandmother	
48	1	1	6	Father		X	
Total: 22	1.5	57 / 2.6	12.5		7	7	

[a](p) means pregnant.

Table 3-14
Questionnaire Administered to Female Prisoners: Contacts with the Family

No.	Do You Keep in Touch with Your Family? Yes	No	Do You Exchange Letters? Yes	No	Who Writes to You?[a]	Does Your Family Visit You? Yes	No	Who Comes to Visit You?[a]
27	X			X (27)	C	X		C,O
28		X		X			X	
29	X			X		X		M,H
30	X		X		H		X	
31	X		X		C,O	X		O
32	X		X		M,F,Ch,O	X		M,F,O
33	X		X		H,Ch	X		H,Ch,O
34	X		X		H,Ch,O	X		H,Ch
35	X			X	F (friends)	X		M,Ch,O
36	X		X		C,Ch,O	X		Ch
37	X		X		H,Ch,O	X		H,Ch,O
38	X			X		X		M,Ch,O
39	X		X		M,Ch,O	X		Ch
40	X		X		Ch,O	X		Ch
41		X		X (41)	C		X	
42	X		X		M,C	X		M,O
43	X		X		M,O	X		M,C,O
44	X			X		X		M,Ch,O
45	X		X		H	X		Ch
46	X		X		C,Ch	X		Ch,O
47	X		X		M,Ch,O	X		M,F,H,Ch,O
48	X		X		M,F,H,C,Ch	X		M,F,H,C,Ch,O
Total: 22	20	2	15	7 (27) and (41): Except her companion	6M, 2F, 6H, 7C, 10Ch, 10O	19	3	10M, 4F, 8H, 3C, 15Ch, 14O

[a]M = mother; F = father; H = husband; C = campanion; Ch = children; O = others.

Table 3-15
Questionnaire Administered to Female Prisoners: Antecedents

No.	Place of Birth[a]	Siblings			Age When Married or Living Together	Schooling	Specialization
		Brothers	Sisters	Total			
27	—	—	—	—	—	7 (r)[b]	—
28	—	—	—	—	—	12 (r)	—
29	C	5	4	10	20	12	None
30	C	1	0	2	18	4	None
31	Cit.	6	4	11	18	10	Typist
32	Cit.	0	1	2	—	16	Nurse
33	Cit.	—	—	11	15	10	Stenographer
34	C	—	—	13	16	9	None
35	Cit.	2	2	5	17	9	Hairdresser
36	C	0	1	2	24 (?)	14	Secretary
37	—	—	—	3	—	11 (r)	—
38	Cit.	3	4	8	14	2	None
39	C	1	0	2	32 (?)	7	Hotel work
40	Cit.	4	3	8	—	3	None
41	Cit.	2	0	3	15	8	None
42	Cit.	7	6	14	15	8	None
43	C	5	12	18	18	8	Typist
44	Cit.	5	2	8	19	5	None
45	Cit.	0	2	3	25	10	None
46	Cit.	0	0	1	16	9	None
47	Cit.	1	4	6	17	11	None
48	Cit.	0	3	4	17	8	None
Total: 22	3 Q.n.a. 6 C 13 Cit.	2.5	2.8	6.7	18.5	8.8	12 None 3 Q.n.a.

[a]C = country; Cit. = city.

[b](r) means taken from the prison record.

Table 3-16
Questionnaire Administered to Female Prisoners: Work

	Did You Work Before You Were Married?			Have You Worked Since the Birth of Your Children?		
	Yes		No	Yes		No
No.	Part Time	Full Time		Part Time	Full Time	
27			—			—
28			—			—
29			X			X
30			X			X
31			X			X
32		X			X	
33			X			X
34			X		X	
35		X			X	
36		X			X	
37		X			X	
38		X			X	
39		X			X	
40		X			X	
41		X				X
42		X			X	
43		X			X	
44		X				X
45		X		X		
46		X		X		
47			X		X	
48			X		X	
Total: 22		13 2 Q.n.a.	7	2	12 2 Q.n.a.	6

Table 3-17
Questionnaire Administered to Female Prisoners: Attitudes

No.	Were You Arrested at Home? — Yes	No	Are You a Victim of Society?	A Strong Woman	A Weak Woman	Do Your Children Know You Are in Prison? — Yes	No	Do You Attend Church on Sunday? — Yes	No	Do You Attend Midnight Mass Every Year? — Yes	With the Children	No
27	—		—			—		—		—	—	—
28	—		—			—		—		—		X
29	—		—				X		X	X		
30	—		—			X		X		X	Will take him	—
31	X				X		X	X				X
32		X		X			X		X			X
33	X			X			X		X			X
34	X		X	X		X		X		X		
35		X		X	X	X		X			When he wants to	X
36		X		X		X			X	—		—
37	—		X	X		X			X	X	When they want to	X
38		X	X	X		X		X		X		
39	X			X		X		X		X	They go alone	
40	X			X		X		X		X		X
41		X		X		Doesn't know		X		X	They will go when they are older	
42		X		X			X	X		X		
43	X			X		X		X		X		
44		X			X	X			X			X
45		X		X			X	X		X		
46	—		X			Two out of three		X		X		
47		X		X		X		X			They go alone	X
48		X	X	X		X			X			X
Total: 22	6	10	2 Q.n.a.	11	1	13	5	11	9	9	4 Q.n.a.	10
	6 Q.n.a.		4 Victim and strong			2 Q.n.a.		2 Q.n.a.			4 Yes	3 Q.n.a.
			2 Victim and strong			1 Two out of three					4 Alone	
			2 Neither strong nor weak			1 Doesn't know					2 Later on	

Table 3-18
Questionnaire Administered to Female Prisoners: Children

No.	Do Your Children Live with You?		By Whom?	Where?	Have They Been Placed?		Why?	Never
---	Yes	No			At What Age?	How Long?		
27	One out of four		The prisoner	Their father	13,10,9	5 years	Prisoner in a state of depression	
28	X	X	Their father	Their father	9,7,6,4	9 years	Separation of the parents	
29		X	Father	A friend's family	3½	1½ years	Separation of the parents	
30	One out of two	1 out of 2	Father	Paternal grandmother	4	6 years	Father tried to commit suicide	
31	X		The prisoner	Paternal grandmother	3 months	1 year	Prisoner's first time in prison	
32		X	The prisoner	Maternal grandmother	At birth	6 years	Prisoner's first time in prison	
33	X							X
34	X							X
35	X							X
36	X		S.W.	Five in foster homes; 2 adopted	2½ months	6½ years	Prisoner in a state of depression	
37	X		S.W.	Foster homes	8,6,4,1	9 months	Prisoner's first time in prison	
38	X		—	Foster home	2	1 month	Prisoner in a state of depression	X
39	X							
40	3 out of 4		The prisoner, Adoption Soc.	Nursery, convent, Huberdeau	10,8,?	8,6,4 years	Parents not getting along; poverty	
41	X	X	The prisoner and then S.W.	Foster homes; two adopted	3,2,1, at birth	16,11,9,8 years except the eldest	First time: Separation of the parents; 2nd time: ?	
42	X	X	S.W.	Foster homes	2,1,6 months	2 years	Prisoner's companion used to beat the eldest child	
43	X		The prisoner	Foster homes; one adopted	At birth	4 months	The prisoner had no apartment	
44	X	X	—	Nursery	1	1½ years	Illness of the prisoner	
45	X	X	—	Maternal grandparents	At birth	8 years	Parents divorced	
46	X		—	—	13,11,9	3 months	Prisoner's first time in prison	
47	X							X
48	X							X
Total: 22	13 One out of two One out of four	7 One out of two One out of four	14 One out of two One out of four					

Legend (By Whom?):
4 The prisoner
3 Their father
3 Social Welfare
2 The prisoner and other

Legend (Why?):
3 Depression
4 Separation
4 Imprisonment
5 Other

Table 3-18 continued

No.	Do Your Children Attend School? Yes	No	Do Their Friends Know where You Are? Yes	No	Do Their Teachers Know where You Are? Yes	No	How Do Your Children Rank at School? Poor	Average	Gifted	Very gifted	Are Your Children Examined Regularly by a Physician? Yes	No
27	X			X	–		–				–	
28	–		–		–		–				–	
29	X			X		X	X				X	
30		X								X		X
31		X		X		X					X	
32	X			X		X				X	X	
33	X		X		X					X	X	
34	X			X	X					X	X	
35	X		X		X			X	X			X
36	X		X		X			X				X
37	X		Possibly		X			–			–	
38	X			X		X			X		X	
39	X			X		X				X	X	
40	X		X		X		X		X		X	
41	X		Possibly		Possibly			She doesn't know			She doesn't know	
42		X		X		X					X	
43	X			X		X				X	X	
44		X		X		X					–	
45	X			X		X			X		They are grown up	
46		X	X			X					They are grown up	
47	X		X		X					X	X	
48	X		Doesn't know		Doesn't know							X
Total: 22	16 / 1 Q.n.a.	5	6 / 1 Q.n.a. / 2 Possibly / 1 Doesn't know	11	7 / 2 Q.n.a. / 1 Possibly / 1 Doesn't know	10	1 / 3 Q.n.a. / 1 Average and gifted / 1 Poor and very gifted / 1 Poor and gifted	1	4	7	11 / 4 Q.n.a. / 2 They are grown up now / 1 She doesn't know	4

Table 3-18 continued

No.	Have They Ever Been Gravely Ill?		Have They Ever Been in Contact With			If You Had the Choice, What Would You Like Your Children to Become?[a]
	Yes	No	The Police?	A Judge?	A Social Worker?	
27	—	—	—	—	—	—
28	—		X	—	—	—
29	X					Musician or athlete
30		X	X			Professor and nun
31		X	X			Actress
32		X				Hippy artist
33		X	X	X	X	Engineer
34		X				Lawyer
35		X	X			Professor of karate and hostess
36	X		X			Artist
37	—			—	—	Model
38	X		X		X	Truckdriver, electrician, and secretary
39		X	X			Air hostess
40		X	X	X	X	Mechanic and beautician
41	She doesn't know		She doesn't know	X	She doesn't know	No idea
42	X					No idea
43	X				X	Teacher
44		X			X	They are already working in construction and running a laundry
45		X				Architect and musician
46		—	—	—	—	They are already working (the oldest is an officer)
47		X				Work with inferiors
48		X				No idea
Total: 22	5 4 Q.n.a. 1 She doesn't know	12	9 3 Q.n.a. 1 ?	3 4 Q.n.a.	5 4 Q.n.a. 1 ?	

[a]The first answer is almost always "Whatever they would like to become."

Table 3-19
Questionnaire Administered to Female Prisoners: Financial Situation

No.	How Many Times Have You Moved Since Your Marriage?	Did Your Husband Provide you with: Enough Money? Yes	Enough Money? No	His Whole Salary? Yes	His Whole Salary? No	Gifts Yes	Gifts No	Did Your Husband Drink a Great Deal? Yes	Drink No	Do You Receive Help from S.W.? For You?	For Your Children?	Telephone the S.W.?	Meet with a Services Worker?
27	—	—		—		—		—		—	—	—	—
28	—	—		—		—		—		—	—	—	—
29	2	X		X			X		X	X	X	2	1
30	0	X			X	X			X	X	X	0	1
31	3	X			X	X		X		X	X	4	1
32	She had no husband or companion												
33	0	X		He didn't work		X			X	X	X	0	2 or 3
34	0	X		X		X			X				
35	4	X		X		X			X	X	X		
36	10		X	He didn't work		X		X		X	X	2	When there was a birth and when they moved
37	—	X			—		—	Both were working		X	X	0	One meeting a week for the children
38	5	X		X		X		X		X	X	0	
39	0		2nd	He didn't work		X		X		X	X	0	0
40	3		X 1st		X		X	X		X	X	About ten	0
41	Always moving	She never asked him for anything											
42	2	X		X		X		X		X	X	Often	One meeting a week or every 15 days
43	2	1st	2nd	—			—	2nd	1st	X	X	0	1
44	10	X		X		X			X	X	X	0	
45	3	X		X		X			X		X		
46	—		—		—		—		X			—	—
47	10	X		X		X		A little		X	X		
48	3	X		X		X			X				

Total: 22

- How Many Times Moved: 3.6 — 4 Q.n.a.
- Enough Money?: 13 Yes, 2 No — 3 Q.n.a.; 2 One yes, the other no; 1 She never asked him for anything; 1 She had no husband or companion
- His Whole Salary?: 8 Yes, 6 No — 6 Q.n.a.; 6 the other no
- Gifts: 12 Yes, 3 No — 6 Q.n.a.
- Did Your Husband Drink a Great Deal?: 6 Yes, 9 No — 4 Q.n.a.; 1 One yes and the other no; 1 A little
- Do You Receive Help from S.W.? For You?: 11 — 2 Q.n.a.
- For Your Children?: 9 — 2 Q.n.a.
- Telephone the S.W.?: 3 Q.n.a.; 5 "0"; 1 "2"; 1 "4"; 1 About ten; 1 Often; 1 Two contacts in a year
- Meet with a Services Worker?: 4 Q.n.a.; 1 "0"; 3 "1"; 1 "2"; 1 "2 or 3"; 1 At birth and moving

Like the men, the women who said they had a trade frequently answered that they were not working prior to their incarceration. However, the situation in this regard is not the same for the women as for the men; many of the women prisoners, as well as the common-law wives of male prisoners, stopped working to look after their families.

This capacity of female prisoners to dream, needless to say, does not necessarily extend to their choice of occupation in prison, which is limited, of course, by what is available. However, the fact remains that reading is the predominant choice, as in the case of the men, followed closely by manual work that is not compulsory.

There is much to be said about the importance of reading in the development and evolution of the individual, but according to all the theories today concerning the positive effects of reading, much depends on the type of reading. With regard to the childhood and adolescent years of the men and women in the two groups of prisoners, the twenty-two women stated that they lived with their parents, whereas two of the twenty-six men did not. Concerning stability of residence, eleven of the women said they had often moved from one area of the province to another, which seems to have been the lot of ten of the twenty-six men. Strangely enough, however, during the interviews, neither the men nor the women prisoners emphasized this aspect of the instability of their past. In analyzing their statements, one gets the impression that such moving around did not affect them adversely. However, the common-law wives of the prisoners complained of this a great deal, not so much to comment on their past as to show the difficulties they had to overcome in their lives as adults and mothers of a family.

On comparing the second group of questions concerning the parents of the prisoners, male and female, certain constants emerge. Of the twenty-six male prisoners, with only two exceptions, all said that they lived with their parents, as did all twenty-two female prisoners. Table 3-20 gives the ages at which the prisoners left their parents' homes, according to the statements of both groups.

Of the twenty-four male prisoners, eight could not, or would not, specify at what age they had left home; the twenty-two female prisoners did so with the exception of one. I feel that it is impossible to make any extrapolations on the basis of these data; all that can be determined is that some of the men and women had been placed elsewhere as children, as confirmed by the interviews, whereas others lived with their parents until the age of twenty-one.

The conclusion we must come to is that prevention as practiced in their case, that is, placement outside the family, proved to be as ineffective as parental upbringing had for others. In short, whereas the old adage "the worst family is better than no family at all" is not confirmed, it is just as obvious that placement, as it was practiced in some of these cases, afforded hardly any better results than parental upbringing.

Table 3-20
Variables Concerning the Age When the Children Ceased
Living with the Parents (Classification According to the
Age of Those Concerned)

Male Prisoners	Female Prisoners
7	4
8	6
12	10
14	11
14	13
15	14
16	14
16	14
16	15
17	15
17	15
17	16
18	16
18	16
21	17
21	17
	18
	18
	19
	21
	21

With regard to the work situation of the inmates' parents, in the female group, eight mothers out of a total of twenty-two worked, whereas in the male group, five mothers out of a total of twenty-six worked. The proportion for the fathers who worked is nineteen out of twenty-six for the men and twenty out of twenty-two for the women. It is possible, however, that there is a tendency among the women of this group to show a certain pride in their father's work, assumed or real. We note that even those who stopped living with their parents when very young gave precise answers to the question concerning the type of work their father did. It is also interesting to note that of the twenty-two female prisoners, only one said that she did not know what her father did, despite the fact that according to the interviews, many had had no contact with their fathers for quite some time.

Should we assume from this that the women prisoners attach more importance to the work value than the men prisoners? This is quite possible, for it is confirmed by several studies on the question. The work value being associated in women's minds with stability and protection, owing to a long tradition of men supporting their wives and daughters, it is understandable that the female prisoners would answer this question more completely and in greater detail than the men.

Regarding the type of trade practiced by the fathers of the male and female prisoners, the similarities are obvious, and the same finding applies to the trade the men prisoners said they practiced before their incarceration, as well as that of the husbands and companions of the women prisoners. In short, it can be concluded that these people come from families of similar income.

One significant fact is that in answering the questionnaire, none of the prisoners, male or female, said that their parents were on welfare, although some admitted it implicitly, if not explicitly, during the interview. In short, they consider it normal that they be looked after by society, but not their parents.

Concerning the children, of twenty-two women prisoners, twenty-one declared that they had lived with their children, while for the men, the proportion was eighteen out of twenty-six. Both groups, of course, were selected because they were all people with dependents, particularly young children. This is why the fact that it is mentioned by the prisoners, even when there had been no continuous cohabitation, showed that they considered it important. Where the men were concerned, the average number of children was 2.8 and their age 10.4, for the women's group 2.6 and a slightly higher average age of 12.5.

The answers of the male and female prisoners to the question of where the children were living at present vary considerably. For the first group, the twenty-six male prisoners, who, according to their statements, have a total of seventy-two children of their own or in their care when they are not in prison, have only five children placed outside the home, two of whom are in hospital. One out of the twenty-six told us he had lost contact with his six children (No. 2). In short, although the children of the prisoners generally live with their mothers or the common-law wives of their fathers, the fact remains that during various periods, when the health of the women makes it necessary, some are placed by social services at their request. These placements were discovered through the interviews with the prisoners, but were not mentioned when the prisoners were answering the questionnaire.

In the second group, for the twenty-two women interrogated, the situation seems to be different. Of a total of fifty-five children, the distribution is as follows:

In an apartment:	10 (aged seventeen to twenty-seven)
With friends:	3
With the grandparents:	8
Placed in foster or group homes:	15
Given for adoption:	5
With the father:	14

The average age of the children being higher for the female prisoners (12.5) than for the male prisoners (10.6), some are already on their own: ten out of a

total of fifty-seven. What is much more significant is that for the women prisoners, the total number of children they themselves or social services have
placed outside the home, or who have been given for adoption, is twenty-three
as compared with fourteen who live with their father. In other words, it seems
that contrary to the male prisoners whose wives or common-law wives keep
the family together, the female prisoners often cannot count on the men for
the same commitment and call on their own parents to look after the children.
As we see, eight of the women's children live with their maternal or paternal
grandparents and in one case (No. 31) with the mother of the prisoner's common-law wife.

There are a number of factors to which the placement of the female prisoners' children can be attributed. On the one hand, social workers, like the
personnel at Maison Tanguay, question the prisoners' real attachment to their
children in many cases. These women, singularly young, think of their little
girl or boy as a sort of doll, adored in the abstract, but on their release, when
confronted with the realities, they frequently abandon the child when they
find that they are unable to look after it and at the same time start a new life.

Over and above the human factors of this kind, always debatable, since it
is practically impossible to decide between the woman's emotional motivation
and the weight of social pressure, the reactions of the sociolegal system play
an important role. It is evident that in all cases where the father does not assume
the care of his wife's children while she is in prison, judges, like social workers,
are more inclined to favor placement of the children than when it is the man
who is in prison and his common-law wife has no criminal record and is
unknown officially to the police and the courts. Furthermore, it should be noted
also that according to the answers to my questions, the intervention of the
sociolegal services was solicited by the mother herself, her parents, or her husband, with the exception of three out of twenty-two families, where the women
prisoners told us that it was the social workers themselves who had proposed
and arranged the placement of the children.

On the basis of the data and the interviews, it seems that the child of a
female prisoner is more likely to be placed than that of a male prisoner, not in
terms of preventive policies or the protection of youth, but more because
female offenders are considered worse than male offenders, making the status
of the mother more precarious than that of the father.

Comparison of the data concerning the categories of people who visit the
male and female prisoners also seems significant in this regard (see table 3-21).
It seems, according to the figures in the table, that the bond between daughters
and the parents, particularly the mothers, is stronger than that between mothers
and their delinquent sons. It must be said, however, that several male prisoners
told us during the interviews that they did not want to see their mothers or
fathers in prison because they already had given them "enough trouble." This
was not said by any of the women.

Table 3-21
Prison Visits

Category of Persons	Male Prisoners	Female Prisoners
Mothers	1	10
Fathers	1	4
Husbands/wives	12	8
Living companions	7	3
Children	12	15
Others (men and women friends)	8	14

This difference in reaction is related to the way in which men and women prisoners perceive their own conduct. The men and their common-law wives see it mainly as that of a "weak person," whereas the female prisoners, throughout the interviews, seemed to consider themselves either "victims" of society or "strong personalities" (fifteen out of twenty-two). Almost all the men told us they would try to change their way of life when they were released from prison, whereas the female delinquents, including the nonrecidivists, asserted that "if they had to do it again, they would."

I present the following resumés of the interviews with the women prisoners, mainly concerning the problems of their children, in order to give some idea of the situations in which these youngsters have to live and grow up.

Resumés of the Reports of the Interviews
with the Women Prisoners

It is impossible for me to reproduce the reports *in extenso* considering their length, in addition to the fact that they contain details that could make it possible to identify the prisoners concerned, but that would not really shed any light on the manner in which the children are now being brought up, either by a third party or by various members of the family. Furthermore, being unable to visit them, it is practically impossible for me to have sufficiently precise information at my disposal concerning the husbands, grandparents, foster parents, or adoptive parents. My knowledge of the situations of the children has had to be gleaned from these interviews. I transcribe the resumés of the interviews in the numerical order in which they were carried out.

Prisoner No. 27: "I began to take drugs at thirty-one years of age, when I learned that my husband had had mistresses for more than five years. . . . I began to go out with men who had been in prison. . . . My boyfriend is now in Bordeaux; he visits me accompanied by two guards. . . . During the divorce, I obtained custody of my four children. My eldest daughter was traumatized at the age of eleven by the fact that I was taking drugs. Two others are placed. The youngest lives with her father."

Prisoner No. 28: "Raped at the age of ten, I was placed in a reform school because my mother could no longer control me. At sixteen, 6 months after I left the school, I was married. As things didn't go well with my husband, I began to take heroin. I had eight children. Four died very young, two because of the heroin I was taking during my pregnancy, the other two during a fire in the house. The four surviving children live with my husband, their father. The oldest never took drugs. He tried once, but it made him sick. He works with his father and is engaged to be married. . . . The other three take drugs and have trouble with the law. They have not yet been in prison. The second stole an automobile; he says that since his mother is 'inside' and takes drugs, he does 'the same.'"

Prisoner No. 29: It is the second time I am in prison. One of my brothers is in prison or has just been released. My child has rejected me since the age of three. . . . I used to feel guilty about him. I am not the kind of mother who always looks after a child. . . . My husband has placed the child with a family and pays his board."

Prisoner No. 30: I was married at eighteen. . . . I have a girl of ten who was placed with her paternal grandmother at the age of four. Social welfare pays the expenses. . . . I haven't seen her for 3 years."

Prisoner No. 31: As a child, my brother and I were brought to court at least about fifteen times for theft. . . . My family understands me because my brothers and sisters are already 'in the same boat'. . . . I have a daughter of two who is being looked after by the mother of my boyfriend. . . . My boyfriend is now serving a sentence of several years. . . ."

Prisoner No. 32: "My daughter of six is looked after by my parents. . . . My parents want her to be a lawyer or a doctor. . . . I have already explained to her why she mustn't take drugs, smoke, or drink. . . . She will take them when she is older. . . . I will guide her when she is first learning to take drugs. I know the good and the bad sides, and I don't want my daughter to have bad trips in any old digs with people who know nothing about it. I have already showed her how to make capsules with cocaine; it is more economical than buying them ready-made."

Prisoner No. 33: "My husband is in prison. My cousins and brothers too, occasionally. . . . I have four sons. The oldest is at Berthelet. . . . I myself placed the other three, but its social welfare that pays. . . . They each have their own pot growing in their room and know how to cultivate it. . . ."

Prisoner No. 34: I have five children; the four older ones are on their own; the youngest lives with her father. . . . I have a long sentence to serve. . . . My husband visits me in prison, and my daughter too. . . . not the others. . . ."

Prisoner No. 35: "My imprisonment will not lead my children to become delinquents. . . . They are five and eleven years old. . . . They live with their father."

Prisoner No. 36: Periods of depression. Psychiatric treatment. Has four children to look after. They are way behind in their studies. . . . They have often changed from one foster home to another. "Prisoners like me, who have no family and whose children have been placed in foster homes, all have the same problem; they have no one to bring them the child on weekends."

Prisoner No. 37: "My child was placed in a foster home after the arrest [she and her husband] . . . . She comes to see me in prison. . . . I want to teach her to be feminine. . . ."

Prisoner No. 38: "I have two boys and two girls, of whom I have legal custody. . . . The two boys [thirteen and fourteen] have already been arrested by the police and have been in reform schools. . . . The other two are with their maternal grandmother. . . ."

Prisoner No. 39: "My child is twelve years old. She has been placed by the social services. . . . At the age of two she had already spent the night in a police station. . . . She was living in a foster home where the husband had killed his wife. . . ."

Prisoner No. 40: "I have four children. . . . They have always been in group homes. With the exception of the youngest [twelve years old] , they don't understand a thing at school. . . . They have all been placed in different homes. . . . One of my friends brings the children to prison every weekend to see me. . . ."

Prisoner No. 41: "The man I live with has a long criminal record. . . . Long sentence . . . recidivist. . . . He is married, but wants to get a divorce when he gets out. . . . I have five children. . . . The first two live with my husband, their father. . . . I haven't seen them for 6 years. . . . The other three have always been placed from the time they were three or four. I just learned that my two youngest have been given for adoption. . . . I have never signed any papers. . . ,I don't want them to be adopted. . . . The social worker has been very kind. . . . She tries to arrange for the children to visit me in prison. . . . I never kept them with me very long. . . . They were always placed by me or by the social service. . . ."

Prisoner No. 42: "My children are important to me. . . . My first boyfriend maltreated the oldest girl. My children were placed. . . . I tried to see them again. . . . My boyfriend tried to kidnap them. . . . The Social Welfare Court forbade us to see them. . . but a social worker gives me news of them. My boyfriend wants to get the eldest back, despite the fact that he mistreated her (he once broke her arm while playing), because he is two-faced. In front of people he says he loves his children. . . . "

Prisoner No. 43: "My daughter is adopted. . . . The youngest is in a foster home. The social worker has brought him to prison only once because he lives far away. . . ."

Prisoner No. 45: I had a good childhood. . . . This is the first and last time I'm going to prison. . . . I'll take back my child when I get out of prison and I won't tell him where I've been unless he really wants to know. . . ."

Prisoner No. 46: "My children never knew what I was doing and were never involved in my life of crime. . . . The eldest has an important job in his profession and my two daughters are married. They don't know where I am."

Prisoner No. 47: My son, eight years old, visits his father in the penitentiary and me in prison every 2 weeks. . . . He is in a foster home. . . . He does well in school and is not a problem. When my husband and I get out of prison, we will take the child back."

Prisoner No. 48: "My daughter doesn't know what is happening to her. She is all mixed up. . . . She cries in school, and when she is asked where her mother is, she doesn't know what to say. . . . She was two years old when I was arrested at the airport; she was sleeping and knew nothing of what happened. . . ."

These resumés of the interviews, although very succinct, nonetheless clearly illustrate one of the basic problems concerning the placement of the children of female prisoners in foster homes. The natural mothers still maintain their legal rights and interfere in whatever way they like. This means that it is practically impossible to decide which has the greatest influence—the positive effects of outside intervention in the interest of the child or the negative effects of the relationships the mothers try to maintain at any cost and whose type of lives are generally not those which favor the proper development of children.

Notes

1. Annual Report of the General Direction of Probation and Detention Centers, Department of Justice, Government of Quebec, 1977.

2. Training center for minors situated near the juvenile court in Montreal.
3. Orphanage where orphans or abandoned children were placed at the time.
4. A training school in Montreal.
5. Name at one time given a district in Quebec City.
6. A training school.
7. A receiving and detention center at the time.

4

Conclusion: Social Prevention and Family Assistance

I have tried in this study to cover the social as well as legislative policies concerning minors. I have tried to show that society's attitude vis-à-vis children evolves according to the socioeconomic needs of the various eras. It is accordingly reflected in the legislation on labor and compulsory education and in the status of the illegitimate child or the single-parent family.

However, the protection of young people, as such, is basically linked with assistance to the family—not only financial aid, as is still the case, but help above all in the upbringing of the children. Consequently, as interesting and valid as the legislation may be in terms of its philosophy and its respect for children's rights, when it is a matter of their protection, it will be ineffective if preventive policies are not put into practice. Thus in Quebec, I am convinced that the new law on youth protection can have the expected results only to the extent that, when applying it, account is taken of the need to first select areas and groups in which prevention is most urgently needed.

Police statistics can be made to include precise descriptions of these areas in time and geographical space for each large city, region, and district.[1] It would suffice to keep a systematic record not of the places where the children commit their offence, but of where they live.

Concerning the target groups, to accept as a valid hypothesis that the prime source of juvenile delinquency is sociocultural and not necessarily economic, although the two may appear to be interdependent, is to accept the need to educate certain categories of parents. In effect, considering the cost of individualized social services, it is obvious that we must select effective and pertinent methods of intervention in order to get the optimum results. Research on the type of life led in certain milieus is therefore necessary, and it is on the basis of this idea that I have undertaken my investigation of the families of men and women prisoners who have children in their care.

My first finding concerns the problems of people who are first- or second-generation residents of the city. Brought up in the country according to norms and values that prevail in a rural context, they had come to the city to seek their fortunes. Their hopes for rapid socioeconomic adjustment dashed, they organized their lives without having at the same time assimilated the values needed to integrate fully and, much more important, to ensure the proper upbringing of their children. The disparity between daily realities and their aspirations, as well as the failures and frustrations that followed, were in no way compensated by the benefits of schooling, and there is every chance that

167

the same will be true of their children. Lacking roots, ambition, a sociocultural model, and a certain vision of the future, the men and women of this group transmit no values or stable norms to their children.

What surprised me, during the course of my research, was that I sought to analyze isolated family members and found that this was a group whose members seek and find one another as if by design. Thus the common-law wives of the prisoners frequently admitted that their first husbands or living companions already had criminal records, as did their other mates. In other words, the mothers renewed the experience, knowing full well that this meant their children would have a natural or adopted father in prison. Almost unanimously, they stress the difficulties the prolonged absence of the man of the house creates for the children, but seem unable to realize that they could have chosen to live with men who were not delinquents. It is impossible in this regard to discuss the socioeconomic determinism involved, for during the visits to the homes, it became apparent that many of the women had a higher rather than lower than average standard of living, the percentage of the latter being relatively small in comparison with the whole sample.

It is not my intention to try to find out if these women particularly like the instability of being emotionally attached to a man who lives a marginal life; I simply record the fact that some admitted that their former husbands were serving their sentences in cells next to those of their living companions.

In short, it is a type of society whose members are known to the courts and who, by definition, live what might be called a "chaotic" existence. It would therefore be logical that particular attention be given to children subjected to the consequences of this kind of instability. The second constant I was able to establish during my investigation was the total absence of any kind of instruction for the parents. Although the prisoners' common-law wives say they are receiving or have already received social aid, only those who were sick had ever met with social workers, and then only at their own request. The male prisoners, for their part, had informed the authorities that they had a family to support, but this did not seem to be considered an indication that they should receive special help, other than having a better chance of getting weekend leaves.

Theoretically, under our system it is considered essential to keep the family together in order to avoid the placement of the children. Similarly, in the case of delinquents, it is agreed that someone convicted of a common-law crime who has a family to which he is sentimentally attached has more chance of reestablishing a normal life upon release than a person who is unattached. One would think a priori that in terms of these two objectives, both officially defined as important, that the socioadministrative system would have provided special programs, but such is not the case.

There is another striking fact. The prisoners' common-law wives, when the need arose, were afraid of losing their welfare checks, but not of having to accept the placement of their children outside the home. The women prisoners, on the other hand, were obsessed with the idea that their children would be placed in foster homes or given for adoption without their being able to oppose such measures.

In other words, one gets the impression of being faced with situations in which social intervention does not consist of helping the parents, but only of satisfying the family's most elementary needs, that is, of finding a place for the children who do not know where to go and who, by law, cannot be left on their own.[2] When the children of a prisoner stay with his common-law wife, nothing is done, but the children of a woman prisoner who does not have a man in her life or parents who can, or want to, take them are placed in foster homes, for the simple reason that they cannot be left in the street.

The existence of children is, by definition, closely dependent on that of the parents. It little matters whether the parents are natural and permanent or temporary and occasional—as long as they provide a home for the children, the community refrains from interfering. We well know that criminal milieus are criminogenic, not for genetic reasons, but because of the almost chronic instability of the family situation. The fact remains, however, that the parents are never held responsible, whereas their children "from the age of seven and even before" may answer before a judge for acts they committed, their only rights being the privilege of reduced responsibility.

This simple fact seems to me all the more important in that it has a great many consequences, not only in terms of legislative and socioadministrative norms, but also in terms of research models that should, in principle, be capable of inspiring future reforms. In the first place, studies in Quebec concerning youth protection and the treatment of juvenile delinquency that are clearly oriented toward an analysis of the way of life and reactions of parental couples are rare. Most examine the characteristics and behavior of children who appear before the courts, and especially of those who are placed in institutions, that is, groups of young people with a past laden with experiences for which they are suffering the consequences.

With regard to a target sample, that of the families of prisoners, for example, the studies are few in number and are oriented toward an analysis of whether couples maintain or break their emotional ties when the man has been incarcerated for a more or less prolonged period. The point of this approach is to determine to what extent the community, in sentencing the delinquent to prison, at the same time unjustly penalizes his wife or common-law wife.

Table 4-1 gives the most recent list of studies of this kind, such as that done by Donald P. Schneller in 1978 in San Francisco, California. As can be seen from the table, only Zalba (in 1964) had thought to examine the emotional relationships that exist between female prisoners and their children, and this in terms of the fact that this type of attachment is often much stronger than that they show or succeed in maintaining toward their husbands or living companions.

Table 4-1
List of International Studies on Prisoners' Families

Name of Researcher	Year	Place Where Research Was Done	Method Used	Sample of Prisoners	Sample of Families
Bloodgood	1928	Kentucky	Interviews and case studies	210	210
Sacks	1938	District of Columbia	Interviews and case studies	23	23
Blackwell	1959	Spokane County, Washington	Questionnaire	80	48
Zalba	1964	Alameda and Los Angeles Counties, California	Interviews	124[a]	124
Morris	1965	England and Wales	Interviews	932	676
Anderson	1965	Melbourne, Australia	Interviews	84	59

[a]Zalba studied the case of women prisoners and their relationship with their children.

In this respect, as in many others, the woman is penalized to a greater extent than the man. In the opinion of the prison directors I was able to question in Quebec, the solitude of the women sentenced to long terms of imprisonment is much more complete than that of the men, whose common-law wives often continue to visit them for years.

In the last study by Schneller, still only in the form of a xerographed report, he concludes, along with other researchers, that the changes that occur in the male prisoner's family during his incarceration are not financial, nor have they anything to do with maintaining social relationships with others. They are the changing or breaking down of the sexual and emotional ties that existed previously between the man and woman.

It seems, as a matter of fact, that the families of prisoners receive financial aid from the social services, often supplemented by some savings previously set aside. In addition, regarding contacts with old friends, Schneller's conclusions are very similar to my own. In this type of society, where the way of life is fairly homogeneous, a prison sentence is not considered a cause for rejection within the group or any reason for not continuing the same close association. This is an extremely important finding.

Thus there is no stigma attached to a prison sentence for adults, for they live in a special milieu, but the children, who associate with youngsters from different milieus at school, may not only be stigmatized, but also excluded from their peer groups, with the tacit approval, moreover, of their teachers and the school authorities. According to the answers I obtained during my interviews with the prisoners' common-law wives, a large proportion of children know where their fathers or their mothers' living companions are, while others guess the truth but do not want it confirmed in their conversation with adults. At the same time, in Quebec at least, the administrative norms concerning the prisoner's right to receive visits from his children are becoming less stringent, and it may be that for humanitarian reasons, and in the interest of the adult criminal, the interests of the children are being sacrificed.

I would like to conclude with the statement that there is much discussion in all circles about class justice, but there seems to be no great concern about justice for adults *versus* injustice toward children. In other words, contrary to its own interests, society prefers to answer the most urgent needs of its adult members rather than focus on the protection of the rights of its future citizens— its children. In itself, and at the moment, this approach is justified by the obvious dearth of resources and the policy of nonintervention in people's private lives, but over the long term, it is infinitely more prejudicial to the community than the destruction of the environment, for example, which is of the utmost concern today in the industrialized countries, and especially in North America.

Like preventive medicine, educational help for parents who do not have a stable existence is of fundamental importance for the social health of the community. The educational assistance provided by law for juvenile delinquents should not be regulated by law, but by socioadministrative decision.

Under the law, the responsibility of parents is recognized only in extreme cases, whereas in most situations it comes under a form of legal arbitration where the rights of the parents are strictly adhered to even when they go counter to the vital interests of the child. The court records reproduced in this book make very instructive reading in this regard. There we find cases where the children of prisoners, for lack of any other solution, are placed in foster homes, but not given for adoption. The mothers or fathers of these children can always reclaim them like a parcel left in a railway station.

To continue to believe that financial aid can compensate for the deficient behavior of the family is evidence of a type of indifference that is socially and humanly unacceptable, for it results in the penalization of the young. To defend the rights of parents to the same extent as in the past through legislation, including that concerning adoption, is to wrong people of good will who love and are ready to care for children who are not their own.

There is proof that adoptive parents will be "better parents" than the natural fathers and mothers. True, it is inhuman to take away the right to raise their children from parents who look after them, but in my opinion, it is even more inhuman to leave young people in families that at times abandon them and at times demand them back with loud protestations of their rights of "ownership."

Since the new Quebec legislation on the protection of young people recognizes the right of minors to be informed and consulted about their fate, the question arises whether in certain cases adoption should not be authorized after consultation with the child. The report on the Quebec civil code provides amendments to several articles in the present adoption law, but there is always the problem of its application. It is no secret that many Quebec families adopt children from other sources because those in Quebec who need a family are not "eligible" for adoption, or because the norms imposed on adoptive parents are unduly severe, never having been updated.

The natural parents are protected first, then a sort of outdated social hypocrisy permits the adoption services to hesitate a long time before accepting a request. During this time, the children are growing, developing, changing, and becoming "dependents" or "delinquents," but no matter. In the area of youth services, like many others, time does not seem to have the same meaning that it does in the life of a child.

Notes

1. For details, see figures 2-1, 2-2, and 2-3.

2. For details, see copies of the court records in chapter 2, under the section Failures Reported.

Bibliography

Anderson, N. 1968. "Prisoners' Families," *Australian Journal of Social Issues* 2(4).

Anderson, N. 1969. "Prisoners' Families," *Australian Journal of Social Issues* 3(1).

Andry, R.B. 1960. *Delinquency and Parental Pathology.* London: Methuen.

Annuaire du Quebec 1975-1976. 1977. Gouvernement du Québec.

Aries, Ph., and Fell, M. 1970. "La démission du père est-elle un mythe?" in *l'Ecole des parents*, Paris, No. 8.

Aubry, J. 1955. *La carence des soins maternels.* Paris: Les Presses universitaires de France.

Bachman, C. 1974. *Détention et famille.* Genève.

Bertrand, F. 1966. Etude sur les valeurs familiales à Saint-Henri. Document non publié, Départment de Criminologie, Université de Montréal.

Burstein, J.Q. 1977. *Conjugal Visits in Prison.* Lexington, Mass.: Lexington Books, Heath.

Crosthewaite, A. 1972. "Voluntary Work with Families of Prisoners," *International Journal of Offender Therapy and Comparative Criminology* 16(3).

Cusson, M. 1974. *La resocialisation du jeune délinquant.* Montréal: Presses de l'Université de Montréal.

Cusson, M., and Laberge-Altmejd, D. 1977. *Les normes de l'intervention auprès des jeunes mésadaptés: Bilan de la litterature.* Unpublished report.

Davies, L., and Cunningham, D.E. 1974. "The Criminal and Social Aspects of Families with Multiplicity of Problems," *Australian and New Zealand Journal of Criminology* 7(4):197-213.

Depiesse-Hannouille, J. and Van Bostraeten, H. 1978. "Une approche radicale de la protection de la jeunesse: Revue," *Déviance et société* 2(3):289-298.

Eldefonso, E. 1967. *Law Enforcement and the Youthful Offender: Juvenile Procedures.* New York: Wiley.

Fedou, G. 1967. Le magistrat de la jeunesse et la détention préventive du mineur. Conférence prononcée en 1969 à la Session de l'Université d'orientation et d'action éducative, Imprimerie administrative, Melun.

Fenton, N. 1959. "The Prisoner's Family." in *Dault Correctional System.* Palo Alto: Pacific Books.

Frechette, M., and LaPierre, J. 1975. Le diagnostic et le pronostic de la délinquance grave. Troisième rapport d'étape (1974-1975), Université de Montréal, groupe de recherche sur l'inadaptation juvénile.

Geismar, L., and Lasorte, M. 1964. *Understanding the Multi-Problem Family.* New York: Association Press.

Gibbs, C. 1971. "The Effects of Imprisonment of Women upon their Children," *The British Journal of Criminology* 11(2).

Glueck, Sh., and Glueck, E. 1962. *Family Environment and Delinquency.* Boston: Houghton Mifflin Co.

Gunn, J. 1973. "Long-Term Prisoners," *The British Journal of Criminology* 13(4).

Kaplan, E.H. 1976. "Recidivism, Crime, and Delinquency: A Psychoanalitic's Perspective," *Journal of Psychiatry and Law* 4(1):61–104.

Kolakowsha-Przelomiec, H. 1975. "Le milieu familial à la lumière des études criminologiques." in *Les problèmes de la criminalité en Pologne*. Pologne: Varsovie.

Kolakowska-Przelomiec, H. 1977. "La délinquance et l'inadaption sociale des mineurs." in *La genèse de la délinquance des adults*. Pologne: Varsovie.

Laborit, H. 1976. *L'éloge de la fuite*. Paris: Robert Laffont.

Laflamme-Cusson, S., and Baril, M. 1975. *La détention des mineurs de la région de Montréal*. Montréal: AMIC.

Leblanc, M. 1968. "Délinquance juvénile à Montrèal (1960-1966)" Université de Montréal, Département de criminologie.

Leblanc, M. 1971. "La probation juvénile à Montréal: Un inventaire du caseload." Université de Montréal, Ecole de criminologie.

Les Cahiers de Vaucresson. 1978. Leur famille et la nôtre. No. 1, Vaucresson, France.

Levy, H., and Miller, D. 1971. "Going to Jail." In *The Political Prisoners*. New York: Grove Press.

Lox, F. 1969. "Le problème des placements." L'Office de la protection de la jeunesse, Bruxelles.

Maisonneuve, J. 1967. "Relation affective et couple conjugal." in *Le groupe familial* (36).

Manheim, H. 1965. *Comparative Criminology*, Vol. 2. London: Routledge and Kegan Paul.

McCord, W., and McCord, J. 1959. *The Origin of Crime*. New York: Columbia University Press.

Meyer, C. 1963. "Individualizing the Multi-Problem Family," *Social Casework* 44(5):267-272.

Ministere des Affaires Sociales, Direction des communications. 1976. *Rapport du Comité d'étude sur la réadaptation des enfants et adolescents placés en centre d'auccueil*. Guide des centres d'accueil de transition et de réadaption du Québec, Tome I, Comité Batshaw.

Ministere de la Justice, Gouvernement du Québec. 1977. *Rapport annuel de la direction générale de la probation et des établissements de détention*.

Morris, P. 1965. *Prisoners and their Families*. London: George Allen and Unwin, Ltd.

Morris, P. 1967. "Father in Prison," *The British Journal of Criminology* 7(4).

Parizeau, A. 1969. *Etude comparative sur les tribunaux pour mineurs: Québec*. Québec: Editeur officiel du Québec.

Parizeau, A. 1969. *Etude comparative sur les tribunaux pour mineurs: Grande-Bretagne, France, Suède*. Québec: Editeur officiel du Québec.

Parizeau, A. 1972. *L'adolescent et la société; face à face*. Bruxelles, Belgique: Charles Dessart.

Parizeau, A. 1974. *Ces jeunes qui nous font peur*. Montreal: René Ferron.

Parizeau, A. 1975. "Les droits de la jeunesse et le projet de loi C-192," *Revue Criminologie-Délinquance juvénile au Québec* 8(1-2).

Parizeau, A. 1975. "Sommes-nous tous des assassins?" *Revue Criminologie-Délinquance juvénile au Québec* 8(1-2).

Parizeau, A. 1976. "Le placement familial de l'enfance." Rapport inédit, Montreal.

Pendelton, J.A. (1972). "Through-Care with Prisoners and their Families in England," *International Journal of Offender Therapy and Comparative Criminology* 17(1).

Philips, A.F., and Timms, N. 1957. *The Problem of the Problem Family*. London.

Rodman, H., and Grams, P. 1967. Juvenile Delinquency and the Family: A Review and Discussion in Task Force on Juvenile Delinquency. The President's Commission on Law Enforcement and Administration of Justice, Washington.

Roy, G. 1947. *Bonheur d'occasion*. Montréal: Beauchemin.

Rzeplinski, A. 1978. L'influence de l'exécution de la peine privative de liberté sur la situation familiale du condamné. Thèse inédite et ouvrage en préparation, Université de Varsovie.

Schlesinger, B. 1973. *The Multi-Problem Family*. Toronto: University of Toronto Press.

Schneller, D.P. 1978. *The Prisoner's Family*. San Francisco: R and E Research Associates.

Selling, A.L. 1976. "The Myth of the Multi-Problem Family," *American Journal of Orthopsychiatry* 46(3):526-532.

Slocum, W.L., and Stone, C.L. 1963. "Family, Culture Patterns and Delinquent Type Behavior," *Marriage and Family Living* 25:202-208.

Steller, M. 1978. "Quelques aspects de la protection des mineurs telle qu'elle a été conçue dans le canton de Genève: Revue," *Déviance et Société* 2(3): 299-307.

Szabo, D. 1960. *Crimes et villes*. Paris: Cujas.

Tait, C.D., and Hodge, E.F. 1962. *Delinquents, their Family and the Community*. Springfield, Ill.: Thomas.

Teindas, G., and Thireau, Y. 1961. *La jeunesse dans la famille et la société moderne*. Paris: Les Editions Sociales Françaises.

Troisier, S. 1976. "Les enfants des délinquants," *Revue Internationale de Criminologie et de Police Technique* 29(1).

Van Nuland, J. 1970. "Les enfants des détenus," *Revue de Droit Pénal et de Criminologie* Cinquantième année (10).

Veillard-Gybulski, M. 1953. Les relations de l'enfant placé dans une famille avec ses parents et les relations des offices de placement avec les parents d'enfants placés ou laissés dans leur famille en liberté surveillée. in *l'Information au service du travail social* (9).

Verrijdt, J. 1975. *Les familles des détenus*. Genève.

Wilmer, C.R. 1966. "Group Treatment of Prisoners and their Families." in *Mental Hygiene*, Vol. 66.

Wilson, H.C. 1958. "Juvenile Delinquency," *Problem Families in Cardiff, The British Journal of Delinquence* 9(2):94-105.

Wilson Harriet, H.C. 1962. *Delinquency and Child Neglect*. London: George Allen & Unwin Ltd.

Wotton, C. 1959. *Social Science and Social Pathology*. London: George Allen & Unwin Ltd.

Wynn, M. 1964. *Fatherless Family*. London: British Book Center

Zalba, S.P. 1964. *Women Prisoners and their Families*. Los Angeles: Delmar Publishing Co., Inc.

Zemans, E., and Cavan, R.S. 1958. "Marital Relationships of Prisoners," *The Journal of Criminal Law, Criminology and Police Science* 48(1).

Index

Index

About the Translator

Dorothy R. Crelinsten has been working as translator for the International Centre for Comparative Criminology since 1969. Her translations from French to English include articles, research reports in the field of criminology and sociology, and books.

She worked on the translations of *The Canadian Criminal-Justice System*, by Alice Parizeau and Denis Szabo (1979), and *Criminology and Crime Policy* by Denis Szabo (1979), both publisned by Lexington Books.

About the Author

Alice Parizeau, journalist and writer, has been working at the University of Montreal since 1969 as secretary general of the International Centre for Comparative Criminology and editor of the review *Criminologie*. A graduate in both law and economics, she has written reports, essays, and articles, on the subject of juvenile delinquency and the system of justice for minors. Published works by the author on these subjects include the essays "Face à Face: L'Adolescent et la Societé" (Brussels, 1972); Ces Jeunes qui Nous Font Peur (Montreal, 1974); and Le Traitement de la Criminalité au Canada (Montreal, 1977). She is the co-editor, with Denis Szabo, of *The Canadian Criminal-Justice System,* published in translation by Lexington Books (1977).

Alice Parizeau has been a consultant to federal and provincial (Quebec) parliamentary commissions on juvenile delinquency and child protection. She received a Presidential Citation from the American Society of Criminology for her work with youth and underprivileged children as cofounder of the Societé Québecoise de Protection de L'Enfance et la Jeunesse, a volunteer community organization.